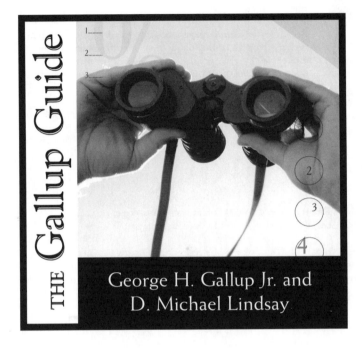

THE Gallup Guide

George H. Gallup Jr. and D. Michael Lindsay

Reality Check for 21st Century Churches

The Gallup Organization
Princeton, New Jersey

Loveland, Colorado

Group's R.E.A.L. Guarantee to you:

This Group resource incorporates our R.E.A.L. approach to ministry—one that encourages long-term retention and life transformation. It's ministry that's:

Relational
Because learner-to-learner interaction enhances learning and builds Christian friendships.

Experiential
Because what learners experience through discussion and action sticks with them up to 9 times longer than what they simply hear or read.

Applicable
Because the aim of Christian education is to equip learners to be both hearers and doers of God's Word.

Learner-based
Because learners understand and retain more when the learning process takes into consideration how they learn best.

The Gallup Guide: Reality Check for 21st Century Churches
Copyright © 2002 George H. Gallup Jr. and D. Michael Lindsay

All rights reserved. No part of this book may be reproduced in any manner whatsoever without prior written permission from the publisher, except where noted in the text and in the case of brief quotations embodied in critical articles and reviews. For information, write Permissions, Group Publishing, Inc., Dept. PD, P.O. Box 481, Loveland, CO 80539.

Visit our Web site: **www.grouppublishing.com**

Credits
Editor: Dave Thornton
Chief Creative Officer: Joani Schultz
Copy Editor: Lyndsay E. Gerwing
Art Director: Sharon Anderson
Computer Graphic Artists: Susan Tripp and Stephen Beer
Cover Art Director: Jeff A. Storm
Cover Photography: Daniel Treat
Production Manager: Peggy Naylor

Unless otherwise noted, Scripture taken from the HOLY BIBLE, NEW INTERNATIONAL VERSION®. Copyright © 1973, 1978, 1984 by International Bible Society. Used by permission of Zondervan Publishing House. All rights reserved.

Library of Congress Cataloging-in-Publication Data
Gallup, George, 1930-
   The Gallup guide : reality check for 21st century churches / by George
H. Gallup Jr. and D. Michael Lindsay. p. cm.
   ISBN 0-7644-2397-5 (pbk. : alk. paper)
   1. Church management—Public opinion. I. Lindsay, D. Michael. II. Title.

BV652 .G26 2002
277.3'083'0723--dc21

                                         2002004951

10 9 8 7 6 5 4 3 2   11 10 09 08 07 06 05 04 03 02
Printed in the United States of America.

Dedication and Acknowledgments

From George:

I would like to express my appreciation to Russell D. Bredholt, who shared with me the vision for this project a number of years ago, for his continuing input. I would also like to thank Michael Lindsay, my partner in many projects, for his painstaking work in bringing this project to completion. I am grateful to Dave Thornton for his calm, gracious, and reassuring oversight of this project, as well as other members of the Group family who have enthusiastically supported this collaborative effort: Thom and Joani Schultz, as well as John and Sue Geiman. Several of the surveys included in this book were written and conducted in cooperation with particular studies and local faith communities. These include projects on the "Unchurched" American, "Faith and the Age Cycle," as well as work with the Mind/Body Institute at Harvard and The Religious Education Association of the United States and Canada. Thanks also to Randy Frazee for sharing a portion of the Christian Life Profile as well as surveys conducted for the Southern New Jersey Annual Conference of the United Methodist Church, the Episcopal Diocese at New Jersey, Trinity Church, and All Saints' Church, both of Princeton, New Jersey. I dedicate this book to Dr. Miriam Murphy, sociologist and Sister of Notre Dame, who has been a spiritual mentor to me for a quarter of a century. And to my wife, Kingsley, and our three children—Alison, George, and Kingsley—who for many years have shared my enthusiasm for exploring the spiritual life through scientific surveys.

From Michael:

I am most grateful to my mentor and friend, George Gallup, for inviting me to collaborate on this project. I also wish to thank the Rotary Foundation and specifically Dr. Lewis Lipscomb, my sponsor as a Rotary Ambassadorial Scholar, for their support and encouragement during my year of study and research at Oxford University when much of this book was written. Their efforts, as well as several special friendships in Oxford, made the year not only productive but also enjoyable. I appreciate the support and input of my Oxford tutor, Alister McGrath, and thank him for his constructive feedback on an earlier version of this manuscript. To my advisor, Robert Wuthnow, and my Princeton colleagues and cohort-mates, thank you for shaping my sociological imagination. And finally, to my parents, Susan and Ken Lindsay—for their unconditional love and countless sacrifices—and to my wife, Rebecca, whose love and support has sustained me through this and every other worthwhile endeavor, with love and appreciation, I dedicate this book to you.

Table of Contents

"The sons of Issachar...

understood the times and

knew what Israel should do."

—1 Chronicles 12:32

Foreword

In the middle of a lengthy list of warriors who agreed to join David in his battle against King Saul, we find a passing reference to an apparently extraordinary group of people, the sons of Issachar. These men, who we surmise had the spiritual discernment to perceive God's hand upon David, wisely chose the proper course of action at a pivotal moment in Israel's history. What an arresting testimony! These men not only discerned the "signs of the times" but also knew how to respond. At the dawn of a new century—when churches and their leaders need to take the spiritual pulse of their own congregations and communities—we need a new generation of the sons of Issachar. We need a generation of spiritual leaders who can wisely perceive God's vision for his people and who can resolve to bring that vision into reality.

It is to this aim that we offer this book as a tool to assist twenty-first century church leaders in becoming sons of Issachar in our own time.

Survey research surrounds us. The Constitution of the United States of America specifies a decennial census, a survey every ten years that provides us with a wealth of information, including population trends that help apportion representation in the House of Representatives. Contemporary society relies on scientific surveys to a remarkable extent. From political opinions to market research, from popular attitudes to individual preferences, survey research informs decision-makers about the thoughts and inclinations of their constituents. It is, therefore, not too surprising that church leaders have recognized the value of scientific surveys in guiding their congregational leadership. Before the church sets out on a new course, the minister has to know what the people think and feel about the venture. Church leaders need to discover why people leave the church and how to bring them back. One of the best ways to do that is with a carefully documented survey, conducted anonymously, so that people feel free to give full and frank answers.

Let us be clear: while it is important to listen to your congregation and others, every effective minister must first seek the voice of the Lord. To that end, we suggest that all churches pursue a time of extended prayer and reflection before beginning any survey project. Congregations and their leaders need divine insight as they seek to use the wonderful tool of survey research to further their ministry and mission. If handled properly, this tool can help the minister and church leadership better listen to members of the congregation. It can shed light on the needs of people outside the church and how best to reach them, as well as how best to nurture people within the church body.

It is our prayer that *The Gallup Guide* will enable you to harness the tremendous power of survey research in understanding our times and in knowing what to do in response to God's leadership as you seek to become a twenty-first century son of Issachar.

—George Gallup Jr. and D. Michael Lindsay
Princeton, New Jersey
July 2002

Introduction:
The Lay of the Land

Not long ago I received a call from the clergy person in charge of a large central New Jersey church: "George, I really need your help. Hundreds of newcomers have joined my church over the last decade, bringing with them new ideas, new needs, and new energies. I really feel the need to get a sense of how the people of my church, both the newcomers and veterans, feel about the church today and the direction in which it is headed. Can you help me?"

One of the most dramatic—yet perhaps least noticed—developments of the last decade has been the explosion of interest among the U.S. populace in spiritual matters.

Over the years we have received numerous letters and telephone calls such as this—some with a note of urgency, even frustration—from clergy who seem eager to have a reality check on the needs, physical and spiritual, of their congregations.

In the case of the central New Jersey clergyman, the Gallup team worked with him and a survey team from his church, helping them develop the questionnaire and guiding them in the administration of the survey.

The findings were presented at the church's annual meeting. The head of the church's survey committee commented on the impact of the survey: "The survey was just what we needed at a time when there were lots of differences in different corners of the church. The survey—which, incidentally, brought out issues we were unaware of—provided the collective voice and energy required to accurately identify needs and to set courses of action."

The churches of America, in these opening years of the twenty-first century, face an historic moment of opportunity. Surveys record an unprecedented desire for religious and spiritual growth among people in all walks of life and in every region of the nation. There is an intense searching for spiritual moorings, a hunger for God. It is for churches to seize the moment and to direct this often vague and free-floating spirituality into a solid and lived-out faith.

It is our conviction that scientific survey research can help greatly in this process. We believe that survey research has never been more needed than it is today to help church leaders ascertain where people are in the religious and spiritual growth process and the steps needed to help them mature in their faith.

One of the most dramatic—yet perhaps least noticed—developments

☑ **The challenges to churches in deepening the faith of Americans are great.**

of the last decade has been the explosion of interest among the U.S. populace in spiritual matters. The percentage of Americans who say they would like to experience spiritual growth in their lives has shot up to eight in ten from six in ten in the early 1990s. Looking back over the sweep of the last decade, Gallup surveys have recorded dramatic increases in belief in supernatural, paranormal, and psychic phenomena. Some of these beliefs fall within the belief systems of traditional religions and have reached record highs. The percentage who believe in the devil, for example, has grown from 55 percent to 68 percent over the last decade. The percentage who believe in hell increased 15 percentage points in just four years, while belief in heaven grew 11 points over a comparable period of time.

Paralleling these trends have been increases in the number of Americans who believe that houses can be haunted, ghosts or spirits of dead people can come back in certain places and situations, people can hear from or communicate mentally with someone who has died, extraterrestrial beings have visited earth at some time in the past, and witches exist.

As Gallup surveys have repeatedly shown, many Americans hold both traditional and nontraditional beliefs at the same time.

People are reaching out in all directions in their attempt to escape from the *seen* world to the *unseen* world. Many beliefs and practices are conflicting and overlapping—for example, born-again Christians believing in channeling. Many people say they believe Jesus Christ is the only way to salvation, but in the next breath say there are many paths to God.

Americans, little aware of their own religious traditions, are practicing a do-it-yourself, "whatever works" kind of religion, picking and choosing among beliefs and practices of various faith traditions.

The challenges to churches in deepening the faith of Americans are great. First, many Americans seem not to know what they believe or why. Furthermore, God is popular but does not have primacy in people's lives. We believe in God, but do we *trust* God?

Ample evidence can be found to show that religion or religious faith is broad but not deep. And the public themselves readily attest to this. The fact is, despite the relatively high figures among Americans in terms of attested belief, many Americans have long questioned the impact religious faith is having on individual lives and society as a whole.

America has, of course, much of which to be proud, including generosity, concern for the individual, and resilience. These have been in great evidence in the weeks and months following the September 11, 2001 attacks. But there is also, of course, a less desirable side to America, which damages our image with other nations of the world: child pornography, continuing high levels of crime and gun deaths, widespread child and spouse abuse, alcohol and drug abuse, fatherlessness, and the lack of a sexual ethic. And while divorce is sometimes necessary, it has gotten totally out of hand: Every other marriage today will break up, spreading dysfunction throughout society.

Will religious faith in America have the power and depth to deal with these problems? Much work lies ahead, for a number of surveys show that faith in our society tends not to be a mature or "integrated faith" revealed by a solid commitment to God and lived out in service to others. In one Gallup survey, we discovered, on the basis of a twelve-item scale, that only 13 percent of Americans have what might be called a truly transforming faith (from *The Saints Among Us* by George Gallup Jr. and Tim Jones).

Some observers believe we live in a period of postmodernism that rejects any notion of a universal, overarching truth and reduces all ideas to social constructions shaped by class, gender, and ethnicity.

Faith communities in the United States face no greater challenge than increasing the level of public knowledge and awareness of Scriptures and of their faith traditions. Many know little about their own faith traditions, let alone other religions of the world.

Kenneth Kantzer writes about the challenge to Christian churches: "No church can be effective to bring clarity and commitment to a world when it is as ignorant of its own basic principles as is our church today. And, unless we engage the church in a mighty program of reeducation, it will be unable to transmit a Christian heritage to its own children or the society around it."

While there are, indeed, severe challenges to churches in their efforts to give form and substance to the sometimes nebulous spirituality that we see today, there are also great opportunities.

If the public's predictions hold true, the present interest in spirituality will continue throughout the current century. Americans generally expect there to be a surge in religious and spiritual feelings that will profoundly affect the world scene. This, they believe, will be fed by global communications, discoveries in astronomy, and an expanded life span. These findings are based on a survey titled *Religious Beliefs, Spiritual Practices and Science in the 21st Century*, conducted for the John Templeton Foundation by the Gallup Organization in 2000.

On the whole, the public at this point sees nothing but expansion in the areas of religious beliefs and spiritual practices during the next one hundred years. The data is powerful. Six in ten think that religious beliefs or spiritual practices will change the way we think over the next one hundred years. And by the ratio of four to one, Americans predict that such beliefs and practices will become more of a force in people's lives rather than less. Eight in ten predict that such beliefs and practices will have a great deal or some impact on the course of history.

Eight in ten survey respondents say it is either very or fairly likely that individuals will experience advancement in religious beliefs or spiritual growth over the next one hundred years. They see this happening individually; among families; in the areas of politics, medical research, and education; and in terms of encouraging greater acceptance of religious and cultural diversity.

Seven in ten, according to this survey in 2000, agree that greater understanding between religious groups will lead to more harmony and reconciliation. Most (eight in ten), however, do not think this understanding will lead to one world religion, a finding that undoubtedly reflects views about history, culture, and perceptions of irreconcilable differences in beliefs among the major religions.

> ☒ **The challenges to churches in their efforts to bring the populace to a deeper, more informed and committed level of spirituality or religious faith are indeed formidable. Yet, in the present climate, the opportunities to do so seem unparalleled.**

The challenges to churches in their efforts to bring the populace to a deeper, more informed, and committed level of spirituality or religious faith are indeed formidable. Yet, in the present climate, the opportunities to do so seem unparalleled.

We are a searching, praying population, perhaps as we haven't been for many years, that acknowledges our need to grow spiritually and in our religious faith. We continue to believe that religion and religious faith can answer the problems of the day.

THE TASK FACING CHURCHES

Much of the spirituality today appears to be ungrounded in teachings, tradition, or Scripture. The task for many churches, therefore, is to understand, inform, and direct this spiritual interest and energy into solid religious commitment and into a sincere and living faith that serves others. If churches fail to direct this spiritual energy appropriately, this spirituality could lead to movements that glorify the self and not God.

It is our conviction that carefully designed and penetrating surveys can play a key role in the process of directing spirituality into deep religious commitment, both at the national and local levels.

But are such efforts warranted? What evidence do we have that deepening religious commitment will change individuals, churches, and society as a whole? A mountain of survey data from Gallup and other survey research organizations offers, we believe, such evidence.

HUGE DIVIDENDS

Surveys consistently reveal the close connection between depth of religious commitment and individual and societal health. Religious feelings, for example, have spurred much of the volunteerism in our nation. Remarkably, one American in every two gives two or three hours of effort each week to some volunteer cause. This volunteerism is frequently church-related. No other institution in our society has had a greater impact for the good than has the church. From the church, historically, have sprung hospitals, nursing homes, universities, public schools, child-care programs, and concepts of human dignity.

Churches and other religious bodies are major supporters of voluntary services for neighborhoods and communities. Members of a church or synagogue, we discovered in a Gallup Poll, tend to be much more involved in charitable activity, particularly through organized groups, than nonmembers. Almost half of the church members did unpaid volunteer work in a given year, compared to only a third of nonmembers. Nine in ten (92 percent) gave money to a charity, compared to only seven in ten (71 percent) of nonmembers. Eight in ten members (78 percent) gave goods, clothing, or other property to a charitable organization, compared to two-thirds (66 percent) of nonmembers.

Religion would appear to have an early impact upon volunteerism and charitable giving, according to the findings of a survey conducted by Gallup for Independent Sector. Among the 76 percent of teens who reported that they were members of religious institutions, 62 percent were also volunteers, and 56 percent were charitable contributors. By contrast, among those who reported no religious affiliation, far fewer were either volunteers (44 percent) or contributors (25 percent).

No fewer than 74 percent of U.S. adults say religion in their homes has strengthened family relationships "a great deal" or "somewhat." In addition, 82 percent say that religion was very important or fairly important in their homes when they were growing up. Those who say religion was important in their homes when they were growing up are far likelier than their counterparts to indicate that religion is currently strengthening family relationships "a great deal" in their homes. Interestingly, "moral and spiritual values based on the Bible" far outrank "family counseling," "parent training classes," and "government laws and policies" as the main factor in strengthening the family and is only superseded by "family ties, loyalty, and traditions."

Eight in ten Americans report that their religious beliefs help them to respect and assist other people, while 83 percent say they lead them to respect people of other religions. Almost as many claim that their religious beliefs and values help them to respect themselves. In another study we determined that the closer people feel to God, the better they feel about themselves and other people.

The survey also shows 63 percent stating that their beliefs keep them from doing things they know they shouldn't do. Only 4 percent say their beliefs have little or no effect on their lives. Still another survey shows that Americans who say religion is the most important influence in their lives, and those who receive a great deal of comfort from their beliefs, are far likelier than their counterparts to feel close to their families, to find their jobs fulfilling, and to be excited about the future.

Churches and other faith communities play a central role in the lives of Americans. At a time of fear and uncertainty about the future of our nation and the world, it is reassuring to find survey data supporting the following observations. Churches and other faith communities...

- are places of rest and renewal in a broken and troubled world.
- discourage antisocial behavior and encourage pro-social behavior.
- are places where faith journeys are shared, lives are transformed, and people are empowered for social outreach.

> ☑ **Three felt needs of the populace at this point in history, as revealed in surveys, appear to be a need for spiritual moorings; a need for deeper, more meaningful relationships with other people; and a need to reach out to hurting people on the margins of society. The churches of America are wonderfully positioned to respond to these three deep needs as we move through the twenty-first century.**

It is also important to note that churches, in dealing with a wide range of social ills, greatly reduce what otherwise would be a crushing tax burden for many people.

Given the huge number of faith communities in the United States and the fact that 60 percent of the populace can be found in these places of worship in a given month, the positive impact of renewed efforts to deepen the faith of Americans is incalculable. Churches are no less than the heart and soul of America, where people can reconnect with God and their fellow human beings.

Rev. Virgil Gulker, executive director of Kids Hope USA, has this to say: "We have five times more churches than post offices. If we can mobilize only ten percent of the members for this work in churches in their neighborhoods, look at the impact."

The religious liberty most Americans cherish and celebrate has enabled religion to flourish in many forms and to become a profound shaper of the American character. Religious liberty has contributed vitality and vigor to the American outlook—an exuberance, a feeling that anything is possible—and often, the courage to bring about difficult but needed change in society.

Three felt needs of the populace at this point in history, as revealed in surveys, appear to be a need for spiritual moorings; a need for deeper, more meaningful relationships with other people; and a need to reach out to hurting people on the margins of society. The churches of America are wonderfully positioned to respond to these three deep needs as we move through the twenty-first century.

SIX BASIC NEEDS

Expanding on these three basic needs, we note still others (apart from physical needs for such things as food, clothing, and shelter). What are churches doing to meet these needs?

1. **The need to believe that life is meaningful and has a purpose.** During a time when sociologists observe an obsession with self in America, three-fourths of Americans nevertheless believe it is very important that life is

meaningful and has a purpose. Yet as many as two-thirds of people interviewed in Gallup-conducted surveys believe that "most churches and synagogues today are not effective in helping people find meaning in life." Here is a basic need apparently being only partially met. The fact is, significant numbers of people find churches irrelevant, unfulfilling, and boring.

2. **The need for a sense of community and deeper relationships.** Many factors conspire to cause separateness in our society. At a personal level, there are high mobility, divorce, and the breakup of families. "Radical individualism" continues to have a hold in the religious lives of Americans. The large majority of Americans, for example, believe that one can be a good Christian or Jew if one does not attend church or synagogue.

One of the poignant consequences to this separateness is loneliness. As we have discovered from surveys, as many as three persons in ten say they have been lonely "for a long period of time."

Our churches need to deal directly with the separateness and acute loneliness in our society by encouraging corporate worship, as well as participation in small groups. Many believe that small groups, rooted in prayer and Bible study, may be the best hope for a renewed church in this century.

Significantly, we have discovered that the closer people feel to God, the better they feel about themselves. They also are more satisfied with their lives than are others, are more altruistic, enjoy better health, and have a happier outlook. Furthermore, we have found that experiencing the closeness of God is a key factor in the ability of people to forgive themselves and others.

3. **The need to be listened to and to be heard.** The main theme in the book *The People's Religion* (by George Gallup Jr. and Jim Castelli) is that religion in the future is likelier to be shaped from the bottom up than by the top down, from the people in the pews rather than by the hierarchy. In a special survey conducted for this book, we discovered that Americans overwhelmingly think the future of the church will be shaped to a greater extent by the laity than by the clergy. Not only do they think it will happen, they believe also that it should happen.

In specific terms this means that, for example, the laity should play a greater role in the church, freeing up clergy to perform what the laity expects of them, which is to listen to people's religious needs and to provide spiritual counseling and inspiration. When the unchurched in one survey were asked what would be likeliest to draw them back into the community of active worshippers, the lead response given was "If I could find a pastor, priest, or rabbi with whom I could share my religious needs and doubts."

4. **The need to feel that one is growing in faith.** Most people want to experience spiritual growth in their lives, as well as growth in their religious lives. The fact is that we go through passages in our faith lives, just as we do in our secular lives. Seven Americans in ten say they have experienced a

change in faith during their life-
times.

It would appear that, basically,
people aspire to lead good lives.
Significant numbers of people
have given thought to living
worthwhile lives, to their relationships to God, to the basic meaning and value
of their lives, and to developing their faith.

> ✓ **What is called for is not new committees, new strategies, or position papers; we need nothing less than changed hearts.**

Churches need to pay close attention to the passages people experience
in their faith lives and to religious experiences which often change the
course of one's life. People need help in understanding the significance of
these experiences and in building upon them.

5. **The need to be appreciated and respected.** This is certainly a basic and
fundamental need, yet as many as one-third of the American people have a
low sense of self-worth or self-esteem as a direct consequence of not being
loved or appreciated. Low self-esteem brings with it a host of social problems, including alcohol and drug abuse, child and spouse abuse, lawlessness,
and crime.

6. **The need for practical help in developing a mature faith.** The clergy often
tend to make assumptions about the depth of religious commitment in the
lives of members of their churches—to assume that their prayer lives are
more developed and that people have a higher level of knowledge about
their faith and the traditions of their denomination—than actually is the
case. Clergy, therefore, can often find themselves in the unfortunate situation of trying to win support for programs and causes from a laity that is
spiritually listless and uninformed.

A close look at where people are in their spiritual lives and the level of
their knowledge would shock most clergy: We read the Bible, but we are a
nation of biblical illiterates. We pray and believe in the power of prayer, but
do not give our prayer life the attention it deserves. We believe the Ten
Commandments to be valid rules of life, but we are unable to name many of
them. We would be hard pressed to defend our faith because we are uncertain about what we believe, let alone why we believe.

We need to work toward closing the gap between belief and practice—
we need to turn professed faith into lived-out faith. What is called for is not
new committees, new strategies, or position papers; we need nothing less
than changed hearts.

Two major challenges face all churches: to reach as many people as possible and to reach them as deeply as possible, to broaden the church itself
and deepen it. Perhaps the deepening process should come first because
parishioners must first be prepared and equipped before they can be effective in evangelistic efforts.

Thanks to the unprecedented level of freedom in the United States, Americans are able to make choices about their future. These choices, many believe, apply most deeply at the religious level: Will we choose the living God, or will we choose the substitute gods of the modern age—money, possessions, fame, drugs, a self-indulgent lifestyle? Will our religion be God-given or man-made?

⊠ **What the churches today do or do not do in seeking to reach our nation's youngest members will have long-term implications in terms of giving young people spiritual moorings for the societal challenges ahead.**

These six basic needs apply to persons in all walks of life and to every age group. Churches need to focus carefully on the nation's youngest citizens since they are tomorrow's leaders—and parents!

SPOTLIGHT ON YOUNG PEOPLE

America's "millennials," persons nineteen and younger, have a very special role to play in the new, post-September 11 world upon us because, as noted, many will soon be leaders, as well as parents. What the churches today do or do not do in seeking to reach our nation's youngest members will have long-term implications in terms of giving young people spiritual moorings for the societal challenges ahead. This is an opportunity that must not be missed.

What are the characteristics of these "millennial" teens (thirteen- to nineteen-year-olds) who will be called on to lead and set the moral tone of society in the decades ahead?

Let's start with some of the more encouraging findings. In our surveys of America's youth, the results underscore the compelling qualities of youth: idealism, optimism, spontaneity, and exuberance. Young people tell us that they're enthusiastic about helping others, they're willing to work for world peace and a healthy world, and they feel positive about their schools and even more positive about their teachers.

A large majority of American youth report that they are happy and excited about the future, feel very close to their families, are likely to marry, want to have children, are satisfied with their personal lives, and desire to reach the top of their chosen careers.

In what ways are young people prepared to build a stronger, healthier society in the new world that is upon us?

- Teens want clear rules to live by; they want clarity. Teens favor teaching values in schools, which half of the schools do now.
- Young people overwhelmingly want to reduce the level of violence on television. Television can be a great force for good, but it's not being realized.
- In the area of sex education, teens overwhelmingly would like to have abstinence taught. Young women would like more help in knowing how to say "no."
- Young people would like to see divorce harder to get. They'd like to see

more premarital counseling. It is estimated that as many as half of new marriages will break up.

☒ We cannot fully understand America if we do not have an appreciation of her spiritual and religious underpinnings.

■ Nearly half of all young people today volunteer. Half of all schools have volunteer programs. A majority of young people would like to see such programs made mandatory. If a child is involved as a volunteer before age eleven, volunteering becomes a lifetime habit.

What must be done to prepare the millennials for the tasks ahead?

1. Restore the status of fatherhood in our country. Forty percent of children go to bed at night in homes without biological fathers. Don Eberly and Wade Horn write, "Father absence is the most socially destructive problem of our time."

2. Educate young people about alcohol abuse. Although not generally acknowledged, virtually every major societal problem has an alcohol component.

3. Put constant pressure on TV and movie producers to produce movies that uplift rather than degrade humanity.

4. Invest in lives of children in direct, hands-on ways such as mentoring and adoption. Everyone should ask, "Am I reaching out to some young person outside my family?"

5. Put character first in schools and homes. How we feel is becoming more important than what we do or who we are. Are our colleges turning out brilliant but dishonest people?

6. Pay great attention to the spiritual life of children. Youngsters with a sincere and healthy faith dimension to their lives tend to be happier and better adjusted than their counterparts, are likelier to do well in school, and are more apt to keep out of trouble.

Surveys of teens, and of persons of all ages, can help identify current mind-sets and lifestyles—an essential step if churches are to minister effectively to their congregants. We turn now to the question of surveys—the limitations but also the benefits that surveys can bring to a faith community.

ROLE OF SURVEYS—NATIONALLY AND LOCALLY

No more daunting task faces the survey researcher than attempting to assess the spiritual health of the population. Yet no task is more important because we cannot fully understand America if we do not have an appreciation of her spiritual and religious underpinnings.

Scientific surveys over the last six decades have shown that the depth of religious commitment often has more to do with what Americans do and think than do many other background characteristics, such as level of education, age, and political affiliation.

Polling organizations already survey cross-culturally on many different "external" experiences. The continuing challenge to pollsters and sociologists is to devise measurements that are useful for understanding people's "internal" experiences as well. And these, many believe, are the most important for understanding and improving life on earth. The "inner life" is one of the new frontiers of survey research in a new era of discovery—not of the world around us, but of the world within.

> ✓ Surveys can provide a reality check for churches, helping them operate on the basis of facts, not assumptions.

We believe that the most profound purpose of modern scientific surveys is to try to shed light on the responses of humans to God and, in so doing, gain a sense of God's purposes for humankind.

Surveys on religion have been sometimes described as supporting "leadership by consensus" instead of "prophetic leadership." Our response is that leaders should lead, not follow public opinion. By the same token, leaders should know all they can about the people they are trying to lead because prophetic leadership does not rule out the possibility that God is leading or speaking through his people.

The spiritual climate of the nation has been examined by the Gallup Poll for more than six decades. In addition, Gallup has undertaken special surveys for more than one hundred religious organizations and denominations over this period of time. Both of us have worked with numerous individual churches in helping them develop questionnaires and undertake surveys.

EMPOWERING THE LAITY

To a growing extent, survey evidence, as noted earlier, indicates the church of the future will be shaped from the "bottom up" rather than the "top down." In one survey we discovered that Americans by a six to one ratio said the laity (the people who attend religious services) should have greater influence in their churches. The ratio is yet higher among young upscale groups, who will provide a large share of the leadership of churches in the future.

Surveys can help open up the communications process in a church. The key role of a leader of a church is to lead parishioners to ever deeper levels of faith. To do this, surveys can be very helpful in shedding light on levels of religious belief, practice, and knowledge—as well as spiritual problems and needs—and to measure the degree of progress or lack of progress.

THE NEED TO LISTEN

In *Between Two Worlds*, the English author and evangelist John R.W. Stott offers this advice about listening: "The best preachers...know the people...and understand the human scene in all its pain and pleasure, glory and tragedy. And the quickest way to gain such an understanding is to shut our mouth...and open our eyes and ears...We need, then, to ask people questions and get them talking...[Clergy] should encourage them to tell...about their home and family life, their job, their expertise and their spare-time interests. We also need to penetrate beyond their doing to their thinking."

One way of listening is to conduct a survey in the congregation or community to find out what people are thinking, what they know, what they believe, and what they see as needs for the church. This knowledge will improve the quality of congregational planning. But it will also improve the quality of communication within the church by improving listening skills and helping people to talk more openly with one another.

> ☑ One way of listening is to conduct a survey in the congregation or community to find out what people are thinking, what they know, what they believe, and what they see as needs for the church.

Survey findings can replace hunches, guesswork, and wishful thinking with objective information. In one sense, a survey can serve effectively as a tool of evangelism, as well as a measurement of faith. It can pose questions that challenge the reader to make choices that can relate to the basic tenets of faith. Responding honestly to such questions has the potential to change a person or to start him or her on the road to change. For many, acknowledging unbelief is the first step toward belief.

Every good pastor, just like any other leader in society, has a sense of the nature and needs of his or her people. But carefully conducted surveys can provide unique and vital information about people that is often hidden beneath the "surface" of everyday conversations and encounters.

This book seeks to give ministers and church leaders the skills to conduct local surveys for their congregations. If conducted properly, surveys are often a valuable corrective to either excessive optimism or undue pessimism. Surveys can also spark insight. Using a church survey can be a constructive and creative experience that can inform and build up the community and generate participation at every level.

Surveys can dispel certain misconceptions but also support what we feel to be true on the basis of intuition or faith. Gallup surveys, for example, have added further support to the following:

1. People go through stages in their spiritual lives, just as they do in their lives in general, although the prevailing wisdom has been that faith is something static.

2. *Belonging* can come before *believing* (a finding underscored by the work of Dr. Al Winseman, Global Leader of Gallup Religion Practice).

3. The deeper one goes into his or her faith, the more tolerant, not the less, one becomes (from *The Saints Among Us*).

4. The quickest way to grow the church is through a program of invitation, assuming that the church nurtures and prepares its people for this role.

5. "Unchurched Americans" are overwhelmingly *believers* but are not presently connected with a faith community.

6. Fewer than 10 percent of Americans are "totally nonreligious"—that is, have no church affiliation and say religion is not important in their lives. The vast majority of Americans are presently churched or have been in the past or will be in the future.

BEWARE OF PITFALLS

One also needs to be aware of some of the pitfalls, including accidental or deliberate misuse of surveys. One obvious abuse of a church survey would be to use it to test the popularity of the local pastor. Another misuse would be for one group within a congregation to attempt to establish its superiority by weighing a survey in its favor, perhaps with biased questions. A survey is not a vehicle for special interest groups or preset agendas, nor should it be designed to assess what will market or "sell" superficial values of church participation. It should not be used to undermine leadership or to isolate a minority within the congregation. Finally, survey research should not be used to build unrealistic expectations. Identifying a priority does not mean that the resources for implementing it are available.

The survey will serve the entire congregation, so this project will be most effective if it is a collaborative effort, achieved through prayer followed by consensus and consultation. The personal interaction that goes into planning, conducting, and analyzing the survey can account for some of its most vital results.

SURVEY LIMITATIONS

Before undertaking a survey, you must be aware of its practical limitations.

- A survey will not always provide you with clear-cut answers unless you are testing something very specific. Surveys are most effective as problem identifiers.

- Survey results do not automatically dictate church policy. For example, a majority of those in a congregation may report that they want to end funding for foreign missionaries; that does not mean the church should necessarily follow this course of action. Findings must be viewed as identifying the need for education and discussion among the congregants. While it is helpful to know the current consensus, decisions still must be made through experience, as a matter of conscience, and with the guidance of church teachings and prayer that earnestly seeks God's will.

- Surveys cannot guarantee success. A survey might find younger church members reporting interest in a film series, yet when the church launches one, many young people may not attend. While the survey pointed in the right direction, it did not automatically answer questions such as the choice of films or young people's assessment of program organizers.

SURVEY ADVANTAGES

While surveys have their limitations, it is our belief that the advantages far outweigh the potential pitfalls. A few of the strengths of a survey are that it...

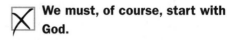 **We must, of course, start with God.**

- assures members that the church's leaders want to know their opinions; it gives them an opportunity to convey their opinions and concerns. This usually also brings an added responsibility: Members expect their leaders to respond to their opinions and concerns, not just "sit on" the results.

- involves the laity in the decision process and workings of the church. Once people become involved, they are likelier to participate in other ways.

- helps set priorities and focus the church's ministry on topics of greatest concern to the membership, current or potential.

- provides information about the congregation's values and priorities in the search for a new minister, pastor, rabbi, or other congregational leader.

- helps discover attitudes toward stewardship, giving, and willingness to volunteer.

- identifies both material and spiritual needs within the church and community. (For example, how many single-parent families are in the congregation, and what are their special needs?)

- provides an early warning system by identifying new problems at the formation stage.

- points out differences of opinion within the congregation that need to be reconciled.

- notes positive trends upon which the church can build and expand.

- provides a system for assessing programs and evaluating progress toward meeting goals.

- suggests ways to reach the unchurched.

- assists in starting new churches by providing timely, relevant demographic data.

- helps compare local congregations with regional and national trends in religious belief and practice.

PUTTING GOD FIRST

This book can be used by persons of different faith perspectives. But the first question that should be asked, prior to any consideration of a survey, is *"What is God calling this church to be and do at this place and at this moment in time?"* We must, of course, start with God. Through prayer and earnest seeking with others in the church, it is important to try to discern God's will for a particular faith community. Set aside time—perhaps a weekend retreat—to seek God's will. What God has in store for you may be something totally different than what you have on your own agenda. Patient and prayerful waiting upon the Lord has, as countless church bodies can testify, set a church off in unexpected directions and into some new and exciting ministries.

☑ **Surveys show that of all the key institutions of our society, the church is the least likely to develop long-range plans.**

It has been said that a church cannot go higher than its vision for itself, yet not infrequently churches ignore this fact. Vision is an act of obedience to God: What is God calling this church to be and do in this place and at this moment in time?

Out of vision—lifted up by the leader and earnestly prayed about by congregants—flow a sense of direction, a focusing of energy and spiritual gifts, and the excitement and assurance that come from seeking to serve God's purposes. A clear vision is also often related to the growth and vitality of a congregation, as well as to increased financial support. And because vision is rooted in the expectant confidence that God is actively involved, it may call for a church to stretch itself in new ways, to take risks.

Articulation of a church's vision can be followed by statements of mission, goal-setting, development of ministry areas, and short- and long-term plans. Such are needed as surveys show that half of churches do not have a mission statement and that of all the key institutions of our society, the church is the least likely to develop long-range plans.

Without an overarching vision rooted in what is believed to be God's purposes, a mission statement to inspire and empower, and long-range plans, churches and other faith communities often are unable to make the vital transition from maintenance to mission.

A FINAL WORD

It is our conviction that surveys can be a vital tool in your efforts to build a healthy church. But a survey is not simply a way to provide incidental information of interest. It should be a call to action—no less is owed all those who gave their time to respond to the questionnaire and those who helped direct the survey. What are the strengths upon which a church should build? What are the major challenges? What specific steps can be undertaken to deepen the faith of congregants? Are people growing in their faith? Are faith journeys being shared? Are members lovingly holding each other accountable? Do people need help in the spiritual disciplines? Are they being prepared to disciple others? Are the gifts and strengths of the members being used for the good of the church?

It is important to be positive. Too often "state of the church" reports reflect mainly the negative. While there is, indeed, bleak news—religion in American society as a whole, as well as in faith communities, is often broad but not deep—it is also true that people with a deep, transforming faith are changing society in profound but often unreported ways.

The faith communities of the United States face enormous challenges, but there are, at the same time, certain factors at work that can improve prospects for deepening religious faith.

To a considerable extent, the soil has been prepared for a possible reinvigoration of religious faith. The United States is, for the most part, a

> God waits for—and longs for—a deep and resounding response from the American people.

"churched" nation. Most people attest to religious beliefs, adhere to a particular denomination, and believe religion is important. Most have had some form of religious training.

Furthermore, the church or organized religion continues to be one of the institutions held in the highest esteem when compared with other institutions of our society, and, therefore, it can be expected to play a powerful leadership role in the future.

Also, churches generally are regarded as having done a good job in meeting the physical and spiritual needs of people in a given community, and the clergy continue to be held in high esteem.

The vast majority of Americans believe in the power of prayer, pray frequently, and believe prayers are answered. The basic foundation for a revitalized faith, therefore, would appear to be in place.

And finally, another basis for encouragement is seen in the fact, as indicated earlier, that rank-and-file churchgoers appear ready to be called upon.

Whatever strategies are developed to revitalize religious faith in our churches and in society as a whole, they should be considered with some urgency. The observation that the church is only one generation from extinction applies today as perhaps never before.

God waits for, and longs for, a deep and resounding response from the American people. It is our hope and prayer that this book will, at least in some small measure, facilitate this response.

Bibliographical References

Gallup, George Jr. and Tim Jones. *The Saints Among Us: How the Spiritually Committed Are Changing Our World.* Harrisburg, PA: Morehouse Publishing, 1992.

The Gallup Organization. *Religious Beliefs, Spiritual Practices and Science in the 21st Century.* A survey for the John Templeton Foundation, 2000.

Lewis, Jo H. and Gordon A. Palmer (foreword by Kenneth S. Kantzer). *What Every Christian Should Know.* Wheaton, IL: Victor Books, 1989.

Princeton Religion Research Center. Emerging Trends; April 1979; June 1980; June 1989; May 1994; June, July 1996; March 1997; April-May, December 1998; April, May, June, November, December 1999; January, April, September 2000.

Stott, John R.W. *Between Two Worlds: The Challenge of Preaching Today*. Grand Rapids, MI: William B. Eerdmans Publishing Company, 1994.

Van Kolken, Paul. "Minister will offer Advice to Bush." The Holland Sentinel; January 28, 2001.

Chapter One:

Getting Started

Any successful survey is composed of eight essential elements:

1. Design. It is important to have clear agreement on the issues to be addressed and why they should be explored. Determine whether a survey will provide valuable information not available otherwise.

2. Planning. Have a clearly defined plan and schedule for seeing the survey through to completion.

3. The sample. This should be representative of the population being studied. However, since most churches have fewer than 250 members, it may be more efficient to interview everyone rather than to draw a sample from the membership.

4. Data collection. How will the information be collected: through in-person interviews, telephone, mail, or questionnaires distributed at the time of the religious services? Interviewers should be carefully instructed on how to contact and interview people in a friendly and unbiased manner.

5. The questionnaire. This should be carefully tested to ensure that the questions are free of bias and elicit the information sought. Sample questions are available in this book, which will be of great help to your survey team.

6. Analysis. Examine the data from every angle, looking at the background characteristics and cross-tabulations (that is, seeing how the results of one question relate to those of another).

7. Report. Present the findings clearly, including details about the survey, so that there will be no misrepresentation of the data and so that an action plan can result.

8. Action. Explore the implications of the findings as a basis for taking action, and apply the findings to policy and practice.

The most important elements of a survey are those in which the church's leadership is already the expert: determining the need for information and applying the information that has been collected.

In this book we seek to provide the church leader with simple, practical, established methods of accurately and inexpensively uncovering important information about his or her congregation and those who come into contact with it, as well as those yet unreached by the church. This book will help the church leader determine if a survey is needed in a particular situation and, if so, how to design and develop a survey questionnaire, as well as discover how to analyze the results. We assume that the more technical phases of a survey project, such as designing the sample or programming a computer to tabulate the results, will be handled by professionals with training and experience in survey research and its methods, if they are required for the project. However, the most important elements of a survey are those in which the church's leadership is already the expert: determining the need for information and applying the information that has been collected.

Every survey begins with a question: "What do we need to know, and why?" When considering a survey, one should first outline the goals and plan the process carefully. A good survey plan answers these questions:

◆ What is the survey's purpose?

◆ What do we want to learn?

◆ What decisions do we want to make for which we need better information?

◆ Is a survey the best way to go, or is the information already available from another source?

◆ What is the target group or groups: church members (active and inactive), the unchurched, the community at large, community leaders?

◆ What method—telephone, in-person, mail, or a combination of methods—should we use to collect the necessary information?

◆ How much money and time should we allocate for this project?

◆ Which tasks can be done by volunteers, and which are better done by an outside professional organization?

◆ Do we have enough qualified volunteers to do the tasks we have identified?

◆ In what way will we make ourselves accountable for the results?

In defining the survey's objectives, one of the most fundamental tasks a surveyor can do early in the process is to create a detailed list of question objectives and an analysis plan of how the data will be used. The guiding principle of questionnaire design is to eliminate any questions for which there is no corresponding objective.

THE SURVEY TEAM

Establish a committee or team to work on the survey. Select church members who can commit the necessary time and energy. Review the plan with them, and invite their comments and ideas; also, decide on how to assign responsibilities for the tasks ahead:

1. Managing the survey: Develop a plan for the total effort and outline time for tasks allotted.

2. Involving the congregation: Define the survey purpose in enough detail to focus questions and analysis. Typically, congregations are likelier to welcome change if they were involved in the planning process. Build consensus within the congregation about the survey's purpose, importance, and results.

3. Designing the questionnaire.

4. Pretesting the questionnaire to establish that the questions and directions are clear and will obtain the desired information.

5. Revising and reproducing the questionnaire.

6. Distributing and collecting the completed interviews or questionnaires.

7. Preparing the data for analysis.

8. Analyzing the results.

9. Drafting a written report of the results and developing strategies for implementing the findings.

Each of these steps can take varying amounts of time, depending on the resources available for the project and other factors in the church schedule. Following are some estimated time allocations as a general rule.

SURVEY PROJECT STAGE	NUMBER OF WEEKS INVOLVED
Managing, planning, and involving the congregation	4-8 weeks
Designing questionnaire	2-6 weeks
Pretesting questionnaire	2-3 weeks
Data collection	3-12 weeks (depending upon method)
Preparing data for analysis	2-4 weeks
Analyzing data	1-2 weeks
Reporting the data and transitioning to an action team	2-3 weeks
	Total: 16-38 weeks (4-9 months)

MANAGING THE SURVEY

One person should assume the role of survey director or be appointed. Just as a Christian education program needs a director, a survey requires a leader to make final decisions and to coordinate efforts. Usually, this person also will be responsible for drafting the final report of the results.

The different members of the survey team will help determine how well the survey effort will represent the scope and diversity of your congregation or group. The survey committee should represent both policy-makers and the people who will be expected to implement the results. For example, if you are doing a survey on Christian education, then the committee should include teachers, youth ministers, and others who know the key issues that should be addressed and who have some responsibilities for education efforts.

☑ **It may be helpful to include someone with experience in survey research.**

It may be helpful to include someone with experience in survey research. Depending on the church's location, it may be possible to locate a person who is comfortable and familiar with research methods and the interpretation of survey results. If the church is in or near a university community, you may be able to choose among many people who have experience with surveys. Such a person may be teaching sociology, political science, or communications among the liberal arts faculty or perhaps teaching statistics, marketing, or market research among the business faculty. Others who may be of help are scientists, CPAs, bankers, or business leaders. Incidentally, survey direction and involvement is just the type of project that might appeal to that bright young person or seasoned professional you always wished would become more directly involved in the church's activities.

Once the committee is assembled, agree upon some fundamental parts of the project. The agenda for the first meeting should cover the following:

1. Whom do we interview?
2. What topics should we cover on the survey? (*Note: This does not mean writing the questions, but identifying the issues.*)
3. How are we going to do it?
4. How much money and volunteer time do we have?

You will then want the committee to review the key tasks and agree who will be responsible for carrying out each of these assignments. Set a deadline of two to four weeks for the next meeting when the team as a whole can review the drafted plans, make final revisions, adopt a budget, and set a schedule. In setting the schedule, be careful not to underestimate the time needed to complete the survey. A well-organized survey research organization estimates a minimum of three months from the agreement on the issues to having a draft report in hand. The team will meet as often as needed while the survey is underway and then again once or more when the survey is tabulated to determine how to interpret, disseminate, and implement the results.

A WORD ABOUT SURVEY COSTS

Usually, smaller surveys, such as those undertaken by most churches, incur a higher cost per respondent than larger surveys. Economies of scale suggest that both small and large surveys incur certain costs, regardless of the number of people to be surveyed. These costs are generally acquired during the planning stage (designing the survey instrument), during the data analysis stage, and while drafting the final report.

THE SAMPLE: WHO WILL BE INTERVIEWED

The target population must be clearly defined; it may be composed of a particular demographic profile, such as church members, or those residing in a certain geographical area, such as the church's neighborhood. Professional organizations that survey large populations use various methods to construct and analyze samples to ensure they are representative of the population. The basic principle of probability sampling states that a randomly selected, small percent of a population of people *can* represent the opinions of all of the people—if those few people are selected correctly. The goal is to obtain the same results that would have been obtained if every single person of the population had been interviewed in the survey. In order to produce an accurate sample, every single person within the population being surveyed must have an equal opportunity to be sampled.

When Gallup conducts a national survey, drawing a representative sample of the national population is a complicated process. This book assumes that you will *not* be sampling from a large population but will be surveying the entire congregation or all members of a particular segment of the congregation, such as parents of children attending your religious school. In essence, we are recommending a census, which is a survey of an entire population, however that may be defined. If the church needs to sample from a large population, professional assistance is required to handle technical matters that are beyond the scope of this manual. This book only introduces basic principles of assuring that a sample is representative; it does not aim to teach the theory or practice of actually designing and developing a sample.

Who will be interviewed? Be very precise when defining the group to be interviewed. For example, if conducting a survey of "members," does this mean all people on the church's mailing list? those formally accepted as members of the local church? those who made contributions last year? How about people who are on the rolls but who have not been seen at church in several years? The act of discussing who should be included or excluded in itself can be a highly instructive exercise that further clarifies the goals of the survey. Indeed, sorting out people according to their characteristics or behavior can provide useful information without interviewing. The following is one project that may prove helpful in showing graphically the relationship between different types of members and living patterns.

1. Obtain a map of the local area that shows individual city blocks and covers the area served by the church.

2. Mark the location of the church's main sanctuary on the map. Draw concentric circles at half-mile intervals around that midpoint. (*Note: In large urban areas, consider using quarter-mile intervals; in rural areas, greater distances.*)

3. Use map pins to designate member households or other categories. Several colors can be used to provide insight into membership patterns. For instance:

    Blue pins = members for two years or more who are active members

Yellow pins = members for two years or more who have been less active
Red pins = left the congregation
White pins = joined the congregation within the past two years

4. Now step back and observe the pattern of where the pins cluster together and where there are conspicuous blank spaces on the map. Is the church drawing people from the "right side" and the "wrong side of the tracks"? Has it obtained any new members from a new housing development nearby? Why are so many people in a particular neighborhood becoming inactive and dropping out? Look at where the most active members live. Are they located in a particular area of the local community?

5. Continue to update the map periodically to observe the shifts in membership trends and patterns.

For larger congregations, consider first tabulating these categories of church membership by postal codes. Then put pins that represent the tabulations according to postal codes in the map. The key is to visually notice trends in membership and activity. If you are fortunate, the answers to many questions will leap off the map and will be obvious to the members of the survey committee. Unfortunately, it seldom is that simple. Committee members may have very different interpretations of these patterns, or the how's and why's to explain the patterns and clusters of pins will not at all be apparent. Or it just may turn out that there are not discernible patterns. In such cases, a study is needed to discover from the people directly why they are active or inactive members of the church and what can be done to make church more meaningful for them.

DEFINING THE POPULATION

The project must determine *from whom* the church needs to hear. Suppose the church is considering starting a day-care center. Information can be

SPECIFIC RESEARCH OBJECTIVE	RELEVANT POPULATION
What is the projected use of the center?	*Families with children who are members of the congregation, or* *Families with children who are members of the community as a whole (if the center's services will be open to nonchurch members)*
Is there support for this center among church members? Are there alternate programs that might be seen as more valuable to the congregation?	*All church members*

required on any of a variety of relevant issues, each with different implications for the definition of the problem.

Depending upon the specific purpose of the research, it may be important to interview one or more of several different populations—the community at large, the congregation, regular attendees, or some subset of these. If the research has more than one purpose, the survey team will have to be careful to define the population in a way that includes all relevant groups. For example: What ages must the children of a family be in order for the family to be considered relevant for the study? What are the precise geographic boundaries of the "community"? Are church members to be considered as individual adults or in family units? These types of questions must be answered before the next set of research decisions can be made.

SAMPLING

This manual is designed for those who intend to conduct self-administered surveys among all those in the congregation or a particular subgroup of the congregation. The Appendix provides some of the basics about statistical sampling, its advantages, and its pitfalls. These guidelines apply to surveys when only some part of the population, a sample, is being queried, not when surveying all of one group.

Chapter Two:

Collecting Data

How will the team collect the data? Surveys are typically classified by the method of data collection. Professional survey organizations choose among three primary methods—personal interviews, telephone interviews, or mail surveys—and each has advantages and disadvantages. In the past, most professional surveys were conducted by personal interview. In this method, a sample design is developed and trained interviewers go to people's homes, following strict instructions about which houses on which streets to approach.

Today most surveys are conducted by telephone, again using professionally designed samples and with interviewers following strict instructions about the number of times they should try a number and at which times of the day they should call or retry a previously busy number.

Both of these methods, however, demand a good understanding of sampling methodology. If working without the assistance of a professional survey researcher, we advise most churches to conduct their research without sampling. In other words, seek to reach every person in the survey's universe. For example, the survey team may decide to query all members of the congregation. In this instance, the entire church membership would be part of the survey's universe. On the other hand, your church may be considering a relocation and want to solicit the input of an entire neighborhood. In this case, each household in that neighborhood would represent the survey's universe. When deciding among personal interviews, telephone questionnaires, and mail surveys, three types of decisions must be addressed.

1. **Administrative and resource-allocation issues:** How much time and money has the church allocated for the project?

2. **Questionnaire matters:** How many and what type of questions need to be asked?

3. **Data collection matters:** What biases are introduced by the data collection method, and are these acceptable for the project?

It is important to decide during the planning stage which mode of collecting data the team intends to use, because the survey mode has an impact on the length of the questionnaire, the number of anticipated completed questionnaires to process, and even on the types of questions that can be asked. Also during the planning stage, decide whether the church intends to employ a professional survey research firm or to recruit a cadre of volunteers to conduct the interviewing, for either the person-to-person process or the telephone method.

> ☑ **An interviewer can establish a better rapport with respondents, and this generally means that the respondent will stand (or sit) for a longer interview.**

Each of the three possible methods—person-to-person interviews, telephone interviews, and direct mail questionnaires—has strengths and shortcomings. In comparing the three, we will review the cost of interviewing, the length of the interview, the types of questions for which each is best suited, the quality of the information collected, and the characteristics of the sample that emerges from the completed survey.

PERSONAL INTERVIEWS

This is the costliest of the three methods. Both face-to-face and telephone interviewing require interviewers trained in administering the questionnaires and usually also require the cost of an interviewer supervisor. Costs of the face-to-face method also involve travel and time expenditures of the interviewers. Because a personal interviewer can usually complete fewer interviews in a specified time than can a telephone interviewer, having sometimes to travel between interviews, the cost per interview is generally higher than in the other two methods. This increased amount of time necessary to complete face-to-face interviews also means that, unless the team has a large group of interviewers, it will take somewhat longer to complete the survey than if using the telephone mode.

The higher cost of this data collection method is counterbalanced by several advantages. First, an interviewer can establish a better rapport with respondents, and this generally means that the respondent will stand (or sit) for a longer interview. Whereas it is usually not recommended to conduct a telephone interview that is longer than twenty minutes, a face-to-face interview can last up to forty-five minutes or even an hour. This additional time for interviewer-respondent interaction can yield tremendous amounts of information, often unsolicited by the interviewer. This data collection format is especially conducive to open-ended questions, which can provide a surprising number of insights that far exceed the survey's original intent.

For example, many churches decide to relocate in an effort to better serve what the church views as its primary constituency. Suppose a downtown congregation is considering a move to the suburbs. The survey team might ask households in the neighborhood

CODING

Assigning codes in the form of symbols or numbers for each response category for every item on a survey questionnaire. These codes are used for later data analysis.

of the proposed relocation site if they would be likelier to attend the church if it were closer to their homes. Because of the relatively impersonal nature of telephone or mail surveys, respondents are often not as willing to

> **Face-to-face interviews frequently result in respondents offering more information than the survey explicitly asks for.**

volunteer helpful, unsolicited information that is germane to the survey topic. However, face-to-face interviews frequently result in respondents offering more information than the survey explicitly asks for.

In cases in which the interviewer is able to achieve a measure of rapport with the respondent, the conversation becomes more free-flowing and can yield exceedingly helpful information. For example, in a personal interview the respondent might say, "Yes, we would be likelier to attend the church if it were closer to home, but we would also drive downtown and attend the service if it were over by 11:30 so that our son could continue in the community soccer league." Respondents to telephone surveys do not feel as obliged to volunteer information that is beyond the explicit wording of questions. Likewise, respondents to mail questionnaires will rarely take the time to write out additional comments for each question. In this regard, effective personal interviews can provide extremely valuable information, often in the form of unsolicited but helpful advice. It is far more economical to amend the time of a church service than to relocate the entire church, so do not neglect the value of face-to-face interviews! Personal interviews elicit more open-ended responses, but this may or may not be an advantage. Accurate coding of open-ended questions often can be laborious and challenging in terms of consensus.

While the telephone survey method is a better way to ask sensitive and personal questions, due to the impersonal nature of this method, it is also possible to ask such questions during in-person surveys by handing respondents a card or piece of paper and asking them to write the answers and place the completed answers in an envelope, which they then seal before handing back to the interviewer. This visual assurance of confidentiality is reassuring to most respondents and yields a strong response rate—that is, a high rate of participation in the survey—on sensitive or personal matters.

In addition, the face-to-face model allows the interviewer to show the respondent visual displays. This permits the interviewer to show the respondent a long list of items from which he or she can select items that fit his or her experiences or preferences. In a telephone interview, the surveyor is limited by the number of items someone can remember when hearing the list over the phone. Or, for example, the respondent in a personal interview can be given a card that lists four or five

RESPONSE RATE

 The percentage or ratio that measures the degree to which all eligible respondents agree to participate in a survey.

alternatives; the interviewer may ask him to put them in rank order. This is a difficult exercise over the telephone. Also, the in-person interviewer can show the respondent graphic displays, such as different architectural rendi-

❎ **The level of response is typically slightly higher for personal interviews than for telephone or mail surveys.**

tions of a proposed new fellowship hall, to get their opinions of each proposal. All of these are advantages of the personal interview.

The level of response is typically slightly higher for personal interviews than for telephone or mail surveys. In-person interviews can be more effective in contacting hard-to-reach populations such as homeless people or individuals living in an institutional setting (such as a university). Some in these groups do not own a telephone, and mail surveys may not reach them. Hence, personal interviews can be highly effective, especially if the interviewer is able to remain flexible in scheduling appointments.

One must also remember that the face-to-face dimension of this form of data collection can also be a liability. If part of the community being surveyed is not particularly safe, telephone or mail surveys are preferable. At the other end of the socioeconomic spectrum, it may be difficult to reach members of affluent households by in-person interviews because they may live in private, gated communities or because they may travel more frequently. Access to apartment buildings may be limited, which introduces additional response bias.

While there is not a firm rule about this, generally speaking, if the response rate is 50 percent or better, the team is doing about as well as the average professional survey. This response rate can generally be achieved in a face-to-face survey (with the caveats about the possibility of losing respondents in low- and high-income areas for the different reasons just discussed). Response rates for face-to-face interviews are typically higher in smaller communities than in large urban centers.

To achieve a satisfactory response rate, interviewers must make several attempts to find someone at home. Interviewers should make at least three calls before giving up on contacting a household. If the church is trying to complete a survey among a very limited universe, the team may want to require a higher number of calls to increase the proportion of completed interviews. Obviously, inter-

viewers should attempt interviews at different times of the day and different days of the week than they made on the original try. If no one was home at, say, 2:00 p.m. on Monday, it is likely they will not be home at 2:00 p.m. on Tuesday, and the surveyor introduces a systematic bias by repeatedly trying to reach the same potential respondent at the same time of the day or the same day of the week. Saturdays are good days to interview since people who work are likeliest to be home this day of the week.

When conducting personal interviews, you are far likelier to elicit responses if the church sends a letter in advance of the interview, informing respondents of the survey's aim and the approximate time frame in which an interviewer will make contact. The

> ✓ **Generally speaking, if the response rate is 50 percent or better, the team is doing about as well as the average professional survey.**

letter should also contain information on how the collected data will be used and an assurance of the confidentiality of respondents' answers. Finally, some communities require permits for any form of solicitation, including surveys. Determine if the community you are hoping to survey has such a requirement several weeks before beginning the data collection. In-person interviewers will likely need some form of identification that associates them with the source and sponsor of the survey. The survey team should equip the interviewers with name tags, business cards, or reference documents on church letterhead to convey the survey's legitimacy.

TELEPHONE SURVEYS

Unlike the personal interviews, which can last up to an hour at times, telephone surveys are brief and succinct, but they can be longer if the respondent's interest is sparked. Yet experience shows that the surveyor will have a better completion rate (the number of people who begin the interview and stay with it until the end) if the interviewer holds the length to twenty minutes. Fifteen minutes is better, and ten is better still.

One must also be sensitive to how much people can remember in an oral interview. For example, if the surveyor wants the respondent to select from among alternatives, expect the respondent to remember no more than four options. One cannot ask telephone respondents to put items into rank order unless the number of items is three or fewer. Some of these drawbacks can be mitigated by redesigning a few of the questions. For instance, if there is a list of ten items or alternatives and the survey team wants to know how people feel about them, in a face-to-face interview or in a

PROFESSIONAL SERVICES FOR TELEPHONE SURVEYS

◆ **Random digit dialing (RDD): a telephone survey sampling method in which a probability of all dialable telephone numbers is selected from the working telephone exchanges in a particular area.**

◆ **Computer-assisted telephone interviewing (CATI): a method of telephone interviewing in which survey questions are displayed on computer monitors for interviewers, who type responses back into the system for real-time data analysis. It allows questionnaires to be tailored to the specific responses given by the respondent.**

self-administered questionnaire, the researcher can ask them to review the list and identify their top three. In a telephone interview, the researcher can achieve much of the same aim if

 Telephone interviewing is best conducted from a centralized facility.

he or she asks respondents to rate each of them one at a time, on a scale of one to five where "1" means they do not like the choice, and "5" means they like it a great deal. Although this question redesign will produce most of the information sought regarding people's preferences, the question will take up much more interview time than it did in the face-to-face or self-administered models. Interviewers tend to develop better rapport in face-to-face interviews, but it is possible to train telephone interviewers to achieve a good level of rapport. As a rule of thumb, questions should be no longer than twenty to thirty words.

Professionally produced samples of telephone numbers come close to achieving the quality of sample designs in face-to-face interviews. While telephone samples have the advantage of reaching parts of the community that are not safe or accessible for face-to-face interviews, they have two drawbacks. First, telephone samples, by definition, do not reach households that do not have a telephone. This can be a problem if the church's community has a number of low-income people without phones because the views of those households will not be adequately represented in the survey. It is not clear that this bias is more or less than the bias introduced in face-to-face samples where some interviewers tend not to venture into low-income areas for safety reasons. Second, ensure that the new listings and unlisted phone numbers are included in the sample. There are a number of techniques that achieve this. A simple one, for example, is to flag every certain number of people in the sample, say every fifth number, and reverse the last two digits of that number. Some of those constructed numbers will turn out to be nonexistent or nonworking telephone numbers, but some of them will help the team contact those previously excluded

A WORD ABOUT TIME

Interviewing should be conducted in the early evening, preferably after dinnertime on weekdays (usually between 7:00 and 9:00) and in the midmorning hours on Saturday (usually between 9:00 and noon). While the purpose of your church's survey project is to gather information, you also want to communicate Christian care and concern for those you are calling, an objective that is often compromised if the interview is perceived as interrupting family or personal time. Hence, the survey team should be vigilant about calling during appropriate hours and express a willingness to call back at a better time if the respondent so indicates. If the interviewer encounters a busy signal, the call should be attempted again in thirty minutes, for the respondents are likely home and on the telephone or the Internet.

from the sample. Professionally compiled telephone samples have more complicated methods for ensuring that new listings and unlisted telephones are a part of the sample. These lists are often available for purchase.

Telephone interviewing is best conducted from a centralized facility. This permits the survey team to monitor the progress and quality of interviewers, as well as answer any questions posed to the interviewer that he or she is unable to answer. If for some reason the church decides to conduct telephone interviews from private locations, the survey team should select 5-10 percent of the respondents to contact following the interview to confirm their participation and to verify their answers to a few random items on the questionnaire. This follow-up might also permit the team to ask these respondents about their level of satisfaction with the survey and any recommendations for further improvement. Interviewing from home can be a wonderful outlet for persons with certain disabilities or shut-ins.

The anonymity afforded by telephone surveys often yields significant results, particularly on sensitive topics. As mentioned before, it is possible to offer respondents an anonymous way to answer sensitive issues or items that might be somewhat uncomfortable for them (such as financial status), but these concerns are even more easily allayed through telephone surveys. When conducting a telephone survey, the interviewers should be careful not to mention their first and last names, for this might introduce bias into the survey. In a small community, the respondent may be more or less inclined to participate or to answer in a particular way if he or she knows the person asking the questions. One easy way to handle this challenge is for interviewers to mention their first (but not last) names and the name of the church on whose behalf they are calling. This creates a personal bond between the respondent and surveyor without unduly biasing the survey.

One of the greatest benefits of telephone surveys is the relatively short amount of time this method of data collection takes. Indeed, it is now the most popular method of data collection. Telephone surveys are much shorter than mailed questionnaires. It is not unusual for the *completion* of a telephone survey to take approximately the same amount of time as needed to *design and plan* a mail or face-to-face survey. The telephone method is, indeed, the fastest method of data collection. As with face-to-face surveys, the interviewers are always required to make a minimum of three calls (at different times of the day and mixing up weekends and weekdays) before they can cross off a telephone number from their list, and five to seven repeat attempts are not out of the ordinary for professional survey firms.

Both telephone and in-person surveys can employ multiple skip patterns, which customizes the survey based on the respondents' answers.

For example, if the survey asks about a person's churchgoing habits, the interviewer can probe for greater

SKIP PATTERN

A sequence technique for questionnaire items whereby a respondent's answer determines if the following question(s) is asked or skipped.

specification if the respondent says he or she attends "every few weeks." The interviewer can also skip to the next item if the respondent says he or she never attends. With the assistance of skilled interviewers, questionnaires for

✓ **If a questionnaire is mailed to a household, the surveyor does not really know who has answered the questions.**

in-person and telephone surveys can be more complex than mail questionnaires.

MAIL OR SELF-ADMINISTERED SURVEYS

The only difference in labeling a survey "mail" or "self-administered" is in the distribution of the questionnaire. Anytime someone fills out a questionnaire by himself or herself, rather than having an interviewer read the questions, it is a self-administered survey. A questionnaire distributed by mail is one form of self-administered questionnaire. A major advantage of this method is that the church does not incur the cost of recruiting, training, or supervising interviewers. Respondents are able to answer questions without interacting with a surveyor, as they are either in person or on the telephone. The cost savings per questionnaire is one of the major benefits of this method of data collection. Mail surveys are also helpful because they allow respondents the opportunity to think about questions before responding and offer chances for them to consult personal records if needed.

However, this method introduces two noteworthy drawbacks. First, when distributing or mailing a survey, the church has no control over who decides to complete and return it. Although the church cannot control this completely in the other two modes, they do involve some personal contact with each potential respondent, which tends to increase the possibility that the original sample will remain intact. On the other hand, if a questionnaire is mailed to a household, the surveyor does not really know who has answered the questions. It could be John Rodgers, the person to whom the questionnaire was directed, or it might be Angie Rodgers. It could also be that John Jr. (age ten) intercepted the questionnaire and filled it out, although you may suspect this when you read that the most pressing need for the church is a DVD player in the church basement! The church has little control over who completes mail questionnaires, which can introduce a response bias into the survey.

Also lost is control regarding the *sequencing* of questions. Sometimes the minister wants to know how someone feels about an issue before he or she "educates" him by introducing other issues. This sequencing is handled naturally in a telephone or face-to-face interview in which the questions are asked in the order in which they appear in the questionnaire. In a self-administered questionnaire, there is nothing to stop the respondent from leafing through the entire questionnaire before answering any of the questions.

With these drawbacks, why would the church consider a mail survey? It might consider this method when wanting to use a survey as part of a community education campaign and the survey team is willing to lose some rigor to achieve the twin aims of education and information. Because a mail survey is much less expensive than in-person or telephone surveys, the church can afford to mail out a larger number of questionnaires. This outreach can bring church concerns into the homes of many people in the

> ☒ **The cover letter has been proven to be an effective tool in raising response rates among participants.**

community. However, expect that the response rate will be relatively low—perhaps between 20 percent and 35 percent, compared to 50 percent or more in the other methods—and remember that this will not yield as representative a sample as a completed survey in the other two methods. There is some evidence to suggest that responses overrepresent people with extreme views. Those in the middle are less motivated to participate, so be careful when relying on mail questionnaires for final decision-making.

A cover letter should accompany the mail survey, and both should be addressed to a specific person or household. The cover letter has been proven to be an effective tool in raising response rates among participants. In order to convey the professional nature of the survey project, the cover letter should be printed on church letterhead and hand-signed by a senior officer at the church, typically the senior minister. Both the survey and the cover letter should be printed on white or cream paper with black ink. Surveys perceived as unprofessional will not receive strong response rates. As is the case with the advance letter for the face-to-face interviews, the cover letter should state who is sponsoring the survey, how the data will be used, when the questionnaire is due (usually within ten days to two weeks), and an assurance of confidentiality.

Mail surveys usually last six to ten weeks, even though your cover letter will request a faster response. Typically, follow-up postcards and reminders are needed to elicit further response. The survey must be simple and clear, because the response rate will be lowered if it is difficult or time-consuming. You might consider including in the cover letter a telephone number that respondents may

A WORD ABOUT STAMPS

 The biggest drawback of mail questionnaires is their relatively low response rate. Interestingly enough, social scientists have discovered that stamps can play a vital role in boosting the survey's response rate. For example, questionnaires that are mailed in envelopes with first-class stamps (as opposed to metered postage) attract more attention and are less likely to be discarded immediately. Choosing a colorful, unusual, and commemorative stamp increases the package's attention even more. Also, we encourage churches to provide return envelopes that are stamped instead of business reply envelopes. While the latter may be cheaper, research shows that people feel that throwing away stamped envelopes that are unused is wasteful. This, in turn, increases their chances of participating in the survey.

use to call if they need further clarification. Very few respondents will actually call, but it might increase the response rate of the survey. Individuals respond to surveys that are relevant to their lives. For example, if the church is considering offering free child care on Friday evenings for parents to have a "date night" out, parents of young children are likelier to respond to the questionnaire than people with no children. Hence, the cover letter must persuade respondents that they have a stake in the matter being surveyed. Unfortunately, far too often church surveys fail to explain how the topic under investigation directly affects the respondent and his or her connection with the congregation. Research shows that the following factors influence the rate of return on mail questionnaires:

♦ organization sponsoring the survey;

♦ attractiveness of the questionnaire (format, page design);

♦ length of the questionnaire;

♦ tone of the cover letter accompanying the questionnaire;

♦ ease of completing and returning the questionnaire;

♦ incentives offered to reply (monetary, gift vouchers);

♦ type of mailing (first class or business reply); and

♦ time of the week, month, or year the questionnaire is received.

Page 41 provides a sample cover letter.

Many respondents think that a mail questionnaire provides them with the greatest measure of anonymity among various methods of data collection. While this possibility exists, most surveyors want to track mailed questionnaires to determine which surveys have been returned. How can the team identify non-respondents if the surveys are anonymous? We recommend that the cover letter not suggest that their answers will be anonymous. Instead, assure participants that answers will be kept strictly confidential. This enables the team to assign a number code for each questionnaire. This code, which can be printed in one of the corners of the first page or on the back of one page, will serve as a tracking device for the questionnaire. With a record of all coded questionnaires and their intended respondents, the team can determine the non-respondents for subsequent follow-up. The team can also send a reminder card to everyone, which is a relatively inexpensive step.

Despite several challenges, a self-administered survey can be highly effective in many specific cases; for example, distributing the questionnaire to the church's staff or to all those attending a church supper. We encourage using this method when you are able to have participants complete the survey in a particular place at a specified gathering. Not only does this control the distribution and collection of the questionnaire, but the surveyor can easily reach these relatively small groups.

The survey team can distribute self-administered questionnaires in several other ways. For example:

1. Distribute the questionnaire to the congregation, and ask them to complete it in some specified period (by the same time the next day, for instance).

SAMPLE COVER LETTER

Cross✝Pointe Community Church
Princeton, New Jersey

Office of the Senior Pastor

1 February 1, 2002

Mr. Ron Ward
3434 Purdue Avenue
Princeton, New Jersey 08542

Dear Mr. Ward:

2   As you may be aware, our community has grown tremendously in recent years with scores of young families moving into the greater Princeton area. Our church wants to explore ways we can minister to these new families, and you can be of great help! We are conducting a survey on the attitudes of our church members. We are sending the enclosed questionnaire to each household represented by our church members, and I am writing to ask you to complete the survey and return it this week if possible.

3   Your answers will be kept completely confidential. You may notice an identification number on the back of one of the pages. This helps us track the questionnaire to know when it is returned. Your name will never be placed on the questionnaire, and all lists containing the names and corresponding tracking numbers will be destroyed once all surveys have been received.

4   We hope to share the results with the entire congregation at our annual spring banquet in May. Copies of the final report will be available at the church following the banquet, or we will be happy to mail you a copy if you prefer. Please find enclosed a five-dollar gift voucher that may be used at our church bookstore as a small token of our appreciation for your participation in the survey.

5   If you have any questions regarding the survey, please do not hesitate to contact the survey team chairman, Mr. Kris Segrest, or me. My office telephone number is (609) 910-1000.

Faithfully yours,

6 Howard McNamara
Senior Pastor

1. Date mailed.
2. Purpose of the survey.
3. Promise of confidentiality. Explanation of identification number.
4. When results will be shared. Token of appreciation.
5. What to do with questions.
6. Personal signature with name and title.

COMPARISON OF DATA COLLECTION METHODS			
	Face-to-face interviews	**Telephone surveys**	**Mail surveys**
Cost	High	Medium	Low
Length of time required to complete the data collection	Medium	Short	Long
Length of questionnaire	Long	Medium	Short
Complexity of questionnaire	Complex	Complex	Simple
Control of question sequence	High	High	Low
Control over environment	High	Medium	Low
Ease with which respondent can answer open-ended questions	High	Medium	Low
Able to use visual aids	Very good	Very poor	Good
Respondent's ability to rely on personal records for survey	Good	Poor	Very good
Able to ask sensitive topics	Fair	Good	Good
Rapport	Very high	High	Low
Good quality, verbatim responses	Good	Good	Excellent
Response rate	High	Medium	Low
Anonymity for respondents	Low	Medium	High
Level of intrusion for respondents	High	Medium	Low
Potential for interviewer bias	High	Medium	Low

2. A personal drop-off method in which volunteers deliver the questionnaires to the homes of those whom the team wishes to have participate.

PERSONAL DROP-OFF METHOD

One effective way of conducting a church survey is to combine some of the strengths of two methods. The personal drop-off method builds upon the strengths of both the mail survey and the face-to-face interview. This method works especially well in particular settings—for example, surveys among those who have recently moved to the community. This form of data collection involves what its name suggests: Once the sample is selected (or the survey universe is identified), volunteers drop off questionnaires at home, explain them, and collect them the next week. This usually helps increase the response rate because the person who drops off the questionnaire may establish rapport with the respondent.

Also, by having a volunteer pick up the completed questionnaire, its completion is almost certain.

Use a map and group all selected households by geographical region within the community. This reduces the number of volunteers needed to drop off and pick up questionnaires. Assign each survey volunteer certain homes to visit. A Friday-Saturday schedule usually works best because most people can be found at home on weekends. Drop off the questionnaire one day, and pick it up the next week. Try to schedule visits for late afternoon or early evening before dinner. Volunteers should know enough about the survey's objectives to answer respondents' questions. They should give respondents a brief explanation about the survey, ask their cooperation in answering all questions, ask them to seal the completed questionnaires in the envelopes provided, and tell them when the envelope will be picked up. Volunteers should carefully record the homes where they left and picked up questionnaires. If the completion rate is low, the survey team will know where to return for follow-up. This method, to be honest, is a highly effective way for churches to get accurate, complete information through the assistance of a cadre of trained volunteers. The cost is relatively low, yet the results can be quite profitable.

TIPS ON CONDUCTING MAIL SURVEYS

If a mail survey appears to be the best way to proceed, there are ways of maximizing the rate of return.

1. Personalize the materials as much as possible, and avoid the appearance of "junk mail." Use quality paper, and avoid the cluttered look of address labels used in bulk mailings. If possible, address the envelopes by respondents' names.

2. Begin with the most up-to-date list possible to minimize the number of questionnaires returned as undeliverable.

3. Explore bulk mailing possibilities with the local postmaster. The post office encourages several specific practices that lessen the time required to process bulk mail. It charges lower rates for those who use these practices, which can cut mailing costs by as much as half.

4. Because mailing lists often include more than one name, such as "Mr. and Mrs. John Rodgers," decide whether the survey is to be addressed to Mr. or Mrs. Rodgers or their son or daughter. At the very least, include a question identifying the respondent's role in the household.

5. Include a cover letter explaining the nature of the study, stressing its importance, guaranteeing confidentiality, and urging respondents to participate.

6. Keep questionnaires relatively short—one page to a maximum of eight.

7. Use mostly or all close-ended questions that people can quickly check off.

8. Use an easy-to-follow format and clear instructions.

9. Use a large envelope to mail the materials so the questionnaire does not have to be folded.

10. The following should be enclosed:

   ◆ the questionnaire,

   ◆ the cover letter, and

   ◆ a return-addressed business envelope (already stamped if the budget allows—it will increase the response rate significantly, and the results will be more representative). Using a regular stamp on the return envelope (not a business reply form or a meter stamp) will increase the response rate as well.

11. Use carefully selected, good, lightweight paper (20 lb. is usually best) and envelopes to get the most out of postage expenses.

12. Avoid mailings during major holiday periods. They usually reduce the response rate since people are likelier to be traveling or are too busy to respond.

☑ **Consider using focus groups for pretest stages of the questionnaire when trying to decide what questions are most salient and simplest to understand.**

A few well-placed, open-ended questions on the survey will be of great use, but bear in mind that to give people a chance to expand on a topic may not be of pressing importance to them. Consider providing a "final comments" section, asking respondents to make suggestions or to raise further issues. People typically do not write long essays, but they often appreciate the opportunity to express themselves using their own words at the end of a formal survey. Additionally, respondents to a mail questionnaire may desire to see how their participation affected the overall study. You might consider adding a statement that reads, "If you would like a copy of the study's final report, please check the box below." This offer may encourage greater participation, and the higher response rate may offset the additional expense.

Finally, an extremely effective way to raise response rates while keeping costs to a minimum is the mixed-mode methodology. This often involves mailing the questionnaire first to elicit initial responses. Then the survey team follows up on respondents who have not returned the mail questionnaires by calling them and offering to complete the survey over the telephone.

DATA COLLECTION METHODS THAT ARE NOT STATISTICALLY REPRESENTATIVE

Be cautious about some often-used alternative ways of data collection that might appear to save time and money. These methods are not surveys in the sense that they can be said to be representative of the groups being studied.

1. *Focus groups in and by themselves.* Focus groups—that is, in-depth group discussions—can provide useful information, but standing alone, they are not

anything more than the opinions of the people who participated in the discussion. Do not underestimate the value of what can be learned from focus group discussions, but do not consider the opinions and attitudes statistically representative of the opinions and attitudes of the population from which the participants are drawn, although they may offer a sense of what is most on people's minds. Consider using focus groups for pretest stages of the questionnaire when trying to decide what questions are most salient and simplest to understand.

2. *Clip-out and mail-in surveys.* Questionnaire forms in newspapers, magazines, or bulletins that invite people to complete them are not balanced surveys because the researcher has no control over who sees the questionnaire and who responds. Response rates for this technique are generally low—1 percent to 10 percent—and this method is vulnerable to "ballot box stuffing" by those who wish to advance a particular cause or viewpoint. A church may want to include this method as part of other survey efforts in part of an education campaign to raise community awareness, but it is not a scientific way in which to poll people's opinions.

3. *Call-in or log-on surveys.* Inviting people to call in their opinions by the telephone or log on their responses over the Internet is simply the electronic equivalent of the clip-out and mail-in survey. It has the same limitations and pitfalls as described above, yet this approach is likely to elicit a higher response rate since there is less work involved than answering and returning a mail questionnaire.

4. *Central intercept interviewing.* This is sometimes called the "mall intercept" because the most usual location for intercepting respondents is at shopping centers, although airports or the main crossroads in town are often used as well. Intercept interviewing does not produce representative samples of anyone other than those who frequent the locations. Indeed, the more frequently people go to these locations, the more chance they will have to be interviewed. This may produce a survey based mostly upon the latest opinions of shoppers and frequent fliers, not necessarily the general population.

SPECIAL PROBLEMS IN DATA COLLECTION: ANONYMITY AND CONFIDENTIALITY

One of the advantages of a survey conducted by outsiders is that it carries a higher sense of anonymity and confidentiality for respondents. Being interviewed by a stranger who is telephoning from many miles away or dropping an unsigned questionnaire into a mailbox to be sent far from home means that some stranger who does not know you will not be able to make personal conclusions based on individual responses. That "shield of protection" does not exist when a person is responding to questions or handing a self-administered questionnaire to a volunteer who lives in one's community. With this in mind, the survey team should take some steps to assure respondents, and others, that their responses will be confidential.

Here are some techniques:

1. Rather than collecting completed questionnaires in group interviewing situations, use a "secret ballot box." This enables people to fill out a questionnaire and drop it in a box to be mixed in with everyone else's rather than handing it to someone who some respondents might imagine will remember who turned in a certain questionnaire.

> ☒ **Estimates of functionally illiterate adults in modern, industrialized countries range from 10 percent to 30 percent of the population.**

2. On mail questionnaires:
   ◆ Tell people not to sign the questionnaire.
   ◆ Do not put any mark on the questionnaire or return envelope that some might interpret as a control number that will identify them. Even such innocuous notations as "Survey Number 315" or "version A" will make some suspicious and will inhibit their response. If you need to discriminate among various survey forms for analysis purposes—such as having one form for parents of young children, another form for parents of teenagers, and a third form for nonparents—change the format of the first page. These minor changes can include different page borders, paragraph shading, or font style. Easily identifiable stylistic changes such as these allow the analyst to categorize incoming questionnaires with ease and do not create unnecessary concern about anonymity on the part of the respondent.

3. On questionnaires containing sensitive questions, consider if the team wants to provide the respondent with a prepaid envelope to mail it back rather than having the interviewer take back the sealed envelope.

4. In any cover letter or in other communications, repeat assurances of the care that will be taken to protect the identities of those who respond.

ILLITERACY

The estimates of functionally illiterate adults in modern, industrialized countries—for instance, people who cannot read or complete a self-administered questionnaire in the official language—range from 10 percent to 30 percent of the population. The problem may be nonexistent in your community, or it may affect many members. The church's survey team should be aware of the potential problem and make adjustments accordingly. If the estimated proportion of illiterates in the group to be studied is large, interviewers should read the questions and record the answers or the survey will reflect only the literate members of the group. People who are illiterate usually are experts at coping and avoiding confrontations about their illiteracy. Frequently,

for example, they will say such things as "My wife [who can read and write] answers those things for us" or "I lost my reading glasses." In the first case, you can respond by saying, "We need opinions of both men and women. What if I did all of the 'grunt' work for you? I will read the questions and do all the writing, and you just tell me the answers." In the latter instance the researcher may respond, "That's no problem. Let me read it for you right now so that we can be sure to have your opinions." The survey team may want to discuss this with literacy counselors who are likely to know where the problem exists and to offer advice on sensitive ways to deal with it.

FOREIGN LANGUAGE PROBLEMS

The same caveats apply to those whose fluency in English is limited, which is increasingly a possibility as more non-English speakers populate our communities. Here are some tips when surveying a community with non-English speakers.

1. If the team readily knows the major languages spoken in the community, prepare an "official translation." When conducting a telephone survey, do not try to use bilingual interviewers who have to translate on the telephone. This method will not produce uniform, objective results. Have a procedure in place by which the interviewer identifies the native language of the person being called. Then have a second interviewer with proficiency in that language call back, using an interview form that has already been translated. This may not be practical for all of the languages the surveyors may encounter, but the team should be prepared for the major group or groups in your community.

2. If the team has prepared a translated questionnaire, check its translation before using it by having another person translate the form back into English. Then compare that translation with the original English version. Resolve any discrepancies before using the translated version.

3. Offer respondents both the English and the foreign-language version. Many will choose the English version even if it is not their native tongue and will be grateful for the offer. Past studies have shown that the response from foreign-language groups is superior when they are offered the option than if they are offered the questionnaire only in their native language.

If major ethnic groups exist in your congregation or in the community, be sure to include someone from those groups on the survey committee, both in designing the survey and in interpreting the meaning of its results.

Chapter Three:
Drafting the Questionnaire

What to ask? Survey committees usually face feast or famine. For some, the idea of doing a survey suggests all of the topics that church members have been worrying about for the past twenty years. The task then is to winnow the list down to manageable proportions.

1. **Set a maximum length.** A self-administered or mail questionnaire should not exceed eight 8½ x 11-inch pages. Alternatively, a telephone survey of fifteen minutes is usually most effective (assume that you can ask about forty substantive, short-answer questions in that length of time, plus several key demographic questions such as age, gender, and family structure).

2. **Ask yourself why information is needed about each topic.** If the only answer is "because it would be interesting to know," the topic probably can be omitted from this study.

3. **What can you do with the results?** If you would not know what to do with the outcome of a question, or if you do not have the means to implement a decision by the group, then the question should be dropped.

4. **If you already know the answer, then the question should be omitted** unless it is to be used in analyzing the response to other questions to cross-tabulate answers.

Famine on the committee occurs when you know there is a problem but you do not know where to begin asking questions about it. For instance, the church's membership has been dropping steadily, but no one can offer an explanation.

DEVELOPMENTAL WORK

Questions can usually be developed by conducting preliminary qualitative research to help in the questionnaire design stage. This work can occur in cycles. Begin by drafting a preliminary list of topics to be included in the questionnaire and reviewing that list with the survey team or committee. It is likely that the first list will be too lengthy, but it is not necessary to delete items at this point in the process.

The next task involves fashioning a questionnaire that "works"—one that is understandable, is not too long, and presents reasonable alternative answers from which respondents can select. The first draft will identify topics that need further clarification in the survey. Often, survey researchers solve problems related to the questionnaire through discussion sessions called "focus groups."

FOCUS GROUP DISCUSSION SESSIONS

The major difference between a general discussion and a "focus group discussion" is that the latter is a more tightly centered gathering—a clear purpose exists for the discussion. In this case, the discussion should be focused around the issues needed for the survey's implementation and success. It is a discussion limited to a small number of fixed issues in a semistructured format. This method is often used by professional survey researchers, with the discussion leader often telling the participants very directly the purpose of the discussion: "We are planning a major survey, and we want to make sure that our questionnaire is covering the important issues and that our questions make sense." In many cases, the focus group discussion sessions constitute all of the research that is required, without a follow-up survey. You might find this is all that is needed to gain in-depth understanding of the issues under discussion.

Professionally conducted focus group discussion sessions sometimes take place in rooms with two-way mirrors (so clients can watch and listen). Participants are recruited rigorously to reflect certain characteristics, with cash incentives for participants, and moderators trained in focus group methodology. A church group, however, can conduct a productive focused discussion session in simpler fashion. You are, after all, interested primarily in learning about the congregation. You are not planning to predict the winning presidential candidate in a national election. The key elements needed are a discussion leader or moderator, a moderator's discussion guide, discussion participants, a suitable place to convene the group, and human or electronic recorders.

THE MODERATOR

For the discussion, the moderator does the following:

1. introduces the topic and asks participants to introduce themselves to the group at the beginning of the session.

2. guides the discussion to cover predetermined topics.

3. encourages all participants to state their opinions and impressions.

4. follows up on important and relevant issues that emerge during the discussion.

5. diplomatically manages the discussion so that it is not dominated by one person, does not get off track, and keeps moving to cover the topics needed.

6. summarizes the group's findings at the conclusion of the meeting and then records these conclusions in a report.

A good moderator is a good listener, accustomed to drawing out shy people, and understands that his or her role is to encourage participants to express their opinions, not interject his or her own views. Teachers, many business people, and social workers can be among those who have learned to exercise these skills. It is best not to use as a moderator someone with a visible leadership position in the church, even if he or she has these listening skills. A moderator who clearly has a personal stake in the results of the focus group is less likely to lead an open discussion.

THE MODERATOR'S DISCUSSION GUIDE

The key principle to remember in developing a discussion guide is that the results from a focus group discussion are not intended to be projected to a larger group, as is often the case in a survey. In other words, the discussants' responses reflect only their opinions, not necessarily those of other people. The purpose of the discussion is to find out "why" so that you can craft sound questions with appropriate response categories. Keep the discussion guide focused on what you need in order to refine the questionnaire. If you feel you know enough about how a question is likely to work, do not include that topic in the discussion session.

List the topics to be covered, and write down follow-up questions that might be asked to cover the topic fully. It is sometimes helpful to estimate the amount of time you think each topic might take in the discussion and note those times next to the topic. Be realistic. For example, if a discussion session involves eight to ten people and they each contribute briefly, eight to ten minutes will be spent on that topic alone. If the topic is particularly controversial, it will probably consume ten to fifteen minutes. A discussion session should be scheduled to last about an hour and a half or two hours. One hour is a little short for a good discussion session, since it usually takes about ten to fifteen minutes to get the group "warmed up" and talking. Even with a discussion session of an hour and a half, only about seven or eight topics can be covered in all. Leave some time—perhaps five or six minutes—for discussion of a topic not listed on the outline. Identifying new issues is, after all, one of the purposes of the discussion session. The outline should be written in a way that will allow the moderator to follow a logical progression of topics while also avoiding a rigid question-and-answer routine that disrupts the natural flow of discussion.

THE DISCUSSION SESSION

Before beginning the discussion, explain the procedure: that there is an outline that you would like to follow, that you may ask them to move on to the next topic so as to be able to cover all that is planned, that they do not need to have an opinion on every topic, and that they will not be quoted by name in any report. It is generally good practice to begin by asking members to introduce themselves briefly so that everyone begins to feel comfortable with one another. Invite the participants to tell the group very briefly how long they have been members of the congregation and to describe their families (or some other noncontroversial topic). Do not introduce what might be the most controversial matter to the discussion until the group has expressed its views on one or two less divisive topics. Give the group a chance to become more at ease with one another.

Sometimes a focus group participant will introduce a new topic before the group has completed its discussion of the topic on the table. Some moderators swing into the new topic and then return the group to the original topic. Others prefer to manage the flow by saying, for example, "That's an interesting topic, and I do want to talk about that with you. Let's finish talking about X first and come back to that idea in just a few minutes." Before the session concludes, the moderator should double-check the outline to be sure that all important topics have been covered. It may also be helpful for the moderator to linger after the formal session has ended. Occasionally, participants, now freed from the formal conversational flow, add a valuable insight that they hesitated to advance during the session or in the midst of their group colleagues.

PARTICIPANTS

The group should have about seven to ten participants. If there are fewer than seven participants, there may not be enough to achieve the "critical mass" that stimulates good discussion. Beyond ten members, the group tends to become unwieldy and each participant feels less responsible to participate. Invite a few more than ten to participate since it is common to have a last-minute conflict that prevents a person from attending.

In general, it is best to have a fairly homogeneous group or at least to avoid extremes. For example, you will understand the concerns of older and younger parishioners better if you convene two groups, each comprised of only one age group, rather than mixing senior citizens and teenagers in one discussion group. You may find, therefore, that the team needs to convene four or five focus groups to get a good sense of the issues to be explored in the survey. As a general rule, we recommend that the survey team identify two or three salient characteristics for the focus group (age, gender, and level of church involvement, for example) and use these as determinants for establishing who participates in each focus group (for example, one focus group involving young women active in the church and a second one for young women not active in the church).

TYPICAL TASKS DURING A FOCUS GROUP DISCUSSION

- ◆ reading the proposed question and then asking participants to paraphrase the question in their own words,
- ◆ asking participants to define terms,
- ◆ identifying any response categories that are confusing or questions that are difficult to answer based on the categories provided, and
- ◆ evaluating the ease with which respondents can accurately recall information asked in a particular question.

SETTING

An essential feature of the focus group session is that it should be free of distractions so that people can devote their full attention to the discussion. Here are some considerations:

1. For membership groups, a meeting room at the church is often ideal. Everyone knows how to get there, and it is a familiar setting that will put people at ease.

2. If for some reason you want to get away from the church setting, a member's living room, dining room, or family room may be an appropriate place to meet. Be sure the family (and the family dog!) are away for the evening, or at least are not popping in and out during the discussion.

3. Most communities have meeting rooms that would be appropriate, such as a meeting room in the public library or at the local high school.

Any of these are appropriate if it can be made private and quiet, has adequate parking, and has comfortable seating. Select a location that is convenient and easy to find. Seating the participants around a table, rather than in individual chairs around a room, seems to work best because it lends an aura of formality and seriousness of purpose to the discussion. Also, we recommend offering coffee, tea, or soft drinks to create a welcoming atmosphere. Name tags are helpful if participants will not know one another. Finally, if members of the survey team are observing but not participating, they should be seated against the back wall of the room to remain as inconspicuous as possible. Of course, the moderator should mention the observers and encourage the participants to ignore their presence as much as possible. In most cases, it is preferable not to have observers present.

Assistance: The moderator needs to concentrate on the discussion. It is usually helpful to have an assistant to greet people, find supplies, monitor the tape recorder, and take care of other logistical details so that the group can devote its full attention to the discussion.

Timing: Schedule group discussion sessions at times when the participants can easily attend. This might mean an afternoon session for senior adults, an evening session for younger adults, or a weekend session for teenagers. Research has shown that an invitation to a focus group is most favorably received by potential participants if the group is scheduled on Tuesday or Thursday evenings, typically from around 5:30 until 7:00. If dinner is included with the discussion, then we recommend a time frame of 5:30 until 7:30. This still permits participants with young children to reach home before their children go to bed.

Payment: Professional researchers usually pay participants for attending the group session. Also, focus group participants usually appreciate a small, inexpensive gift (a book or a tape). A gift is not necessary when conducting surveys on church matters. You might, however, try to help by providing services such as arranging rides or making child care available so that people can bring their children with them.

Recording the session: You will find it very helpful to tape record or videotape the session so that the moderator can concentrate on facilitating the discussion rather than taking detailed notes. Any good recording equipment will do, provided that the microphones can be placed to pick up comments from all participants. Be sure to call participants' attention to the recording and explain the reason. While people are self-conscious about being taped during the first few minutes of the session, the tape recorder soon blends into the background and does not inhibit the discussion. In addition to tape recording, it may also be helpful to have one or two persons involved with designing the questionnaire sit quietly away from the table, listen to the discussion, and take their own notes, but not participate in any way. They, too, soon blend into the background, and they will find their firsthand monitoring important to their understanding of the issues. If for some reason you cannot tape record the sessions, then the observer/reporters are absolutely essential.

Reporting: Often, a detailed report is written about each focus group discussion session. This is more usual when the discussion sessions themselves are the only research conducted. When the discussions are held to help design the questionnaire, the report is more of a summary of what was learned that directly affects questionnaire design. Remember not to quote anyone by name in this summary report.

QUESTIONNAIRE DESIGN

Any survey is only as good as its questions. They must be relevant, understandable, and logically ordered. The way questions are worded is critically important to the survey's success. When Gallup conducts national surveys, we have to be careful of two major bias sources: question wording and question order. Writing a clear, unbiased question demands careful attention and discipline. The dual goals of questionnaire design are to encourage response and to elicit accurate answers.

TYPES OF INFORMATION

 Survey questions relating to matters of faith typically provide four types of information. These include

1. **KNOWLEDGE: beliefs regarding the accuracy of facts, as well as exposure to particular elements of the social context.**

2. **ATTITUDES: how people *feel* about something, their preferences, and their desires.**

3. **BEHAVIOR: what a person has done in the past, is presently doing, or expects to do in the future.**

4. **PERSONAL ATTRIBUTES: demographic characteristics that describe the individual. These include age, level of education, gender, income, marital status, race, political affiliation, and religious preference.**

Each of these is important as a source of information for churches and church leaders. When designing a questionnaire, it is useful to identify which of these four categories of information is sought by a particular question. Often it is important to cover all four types to provide revealing cross-tabulations. Remember that effective questions are closely correlated with the item's objective. Hence, if seeking to learn about a person's behavior (such as churchgoing attendance), be careful of asking a question that measures their attitudes (such as "Is churchgoing important?"). The survey must be developed around a central research idea, so it is important to articulate that idea early on in questionnaire development. This is called operationalization: transforming the research idea into survey items. There are two main types of questions: *close-ended* where the respondent selects one or more specific categories provided by the researcher, and *open-ended* where the survey asks respondents to answer in their own words. The following table summarizes the advantages and disadvantages of both types of questions.

QUESTION TYPE	ADVANTAGES	DISADVANTAGES
OPEN-ENDED	1. Useful when survey team does not know appropriate answer categories 2. Allows respondent to qualify his answer 3. Preferable for complex issues that cannot be condensed into 5-6 categories 4. Allow greater opportunity for creativity in answers	1. May create worthless and irrelevant data 2. Data is not standardized among respondents, making comparisons difficult 3. Coding is difficult and subjective; people may provide answers that are not analytically useful 4. Demand more time and effort of respondents, which may decrease the response rate 5. More expensive for coding and analysis
CLOSE-ENDED	1. Answers are standard and permit easy comparisons 2. Less costly to code and analyze 3. Minimizes number of irrelevant responses 4. Sensitive topics (age, income) are likelier to be answered	1. Answers may not reflect respondents' real opinions but are selected out of convenience 2. Many responses categories lengthens the questionnaire, which may decrease response rate 3. Differences in interpretation by various respondents may go undetected 4. Variations in responses may be artificially eliminated by forced-choice responses

We also offer some general guidelines for questionnaire design. Consider the following recommendations:

QUESTIONNAIRE DESIGN GUIDELINES

1. **Begin with easy, general questions.** Asking easy, non-threatening questions at the beginning of the question-naire puts the respondent at ease, establishes interest, and builds rapport. The first question should generally relate to a fact instead of a feeling or opinion, and the fact should require almost no thought.

2. **Be brief.** Long, complex questions can confuse respondents and produce inaccurate results. Generally, the more words to a question, the likelier that the wording itself will influence the response. Try breaking up a long question into two shorter ones. As a rule, limit questions to no more than thirty words.

3. **Use language everyone can understand.** Don't use theological expressions or church jargon. Phrase questions so that the least literate person surveyed can understand them without insulting persons with a high level of literacy.

4. **Do not assume knowledge.** If you were to ask the question, "Do you approve or disapprove of the recent changes in the Southern Baptist Convention?" some people will answer the question without knowing what those changes were. By giving examples of those changes, people will likely respond only to the examples given. It would be better to ask about attitudes toward specific changes. For example, you might ask, "Do you approve or disapprove of the Southern Baptist amendment to the *Baptist Faith and Message* which excludes women from the position of senior pastor?"

5. **Avoid leading questions.** A leading question suggests an answer: "In order to improve the quality of education in church schools, should teachers be paid higher salaries?" This question presents a widely accepted goal (improving the quality of education) accompanied by the assumption that the means suggested (raising teacher salaries) will accomplish the goal—thus influencing the respondent to answer "yes." Questions should be con-structed to minimize the chance of biasing the respondent's answer by leading him or her to a certain conclusion.

6. **Avoid double-barreled questions.** A "double-barreled" question contains two or more distinct questions but allows only one answer. For example, asking, "Should this congregation carry out more social action and evange-lization?" the surveyor will not know whether an affirmative response means the respondent wants more social action, more evangelization, or both. One easy way to spot double-barreled questions is to look for the

words *and* and *or* in each question. If they
appear, recheck the items to avoid double-
barreled questions.

7. **Avoid ambiguous questions.** A question containing ambiguous terms can be easily misun-
derstood and misinterpreted. For example, the
question "Do you think juvenile delinquents
should be dealt with firmly?" includes the
terms *juvenile delinquents* and *firmly*, which people
interpret in different ways.

8. **Avoid value-laden or emotional terms.** When a question contains a value-
laden term, respondents may answer emotionally, without regard for the
context in which the term is used. If you ask people's attitudes toward a
specific government social program and characterize it as "liberal" or "conservative," people are likely to react to their feelings about "liberal" or
"conservative" and not about the program itself.

9. **Avoid questions with "socially acceptable" answers.** When asked about
their participation in activities such as voting, attending church, or participating in charity, people tend to give socially acceptable answers that
exaggerate their involvement. Only ask questions such as these when you
understand their limitations and when you have a control in the survey to
make the answers more meaningful. For example, if you ask people
whether they read religious publications or watch religious television, use a
follow-up question asking them to name a publication or program.

Church attendance is a particularly challenging item to measure in the
American context because it is laden with socially appropriate norms.
Instead of asking a respondent, "Do you go to church often?" ask him or
her, "Have you been to church within the last seven days?" When surveying a population that does not typically attend church regularly, consider
revising the question to ask, "Aside from special events like weddings and
funerals, approximately how many times have you attended church in the
last year?"

If you want to find out whether people will volunteer to work for the
church, include "volunteer work" on a list of activities for respondents to
choose from. Such a list should be broad enough to include something to
which everyone can say "yes." As an added control, you might ask respondents to describe their volunteer work.

10. **Do not ask about "average" behavior.** If you want to measure church
attendance, don't ask "How often do you attend church in an average
week?" That question asks the respondent to average his or her own
behavior. Instead, ask "How often did you attend church in the last seven
days?" and leave the averaging to the researcher.

11. Tell respondents how specific their answers should be and use ranges where appropriate. If you ask "How long have you lived in this community?" you may get answers ranging from "all my life" to "thirteen weeks." To improve efficiency, provide ranges so people can know how specific to make their answers. Ask, "How long have you lived in this community—less than one year, two to five years, six to ten years, or more than ten years?" Providing ranges can also be helpful when asking personal questions, such as age and income. Some respondents may hesitate to tell you their exact age but will have no qualms about telling you whether they are 18 to 29, 30 to 49, 50 to 64, or over 65.

This advice, of course, is balanced with a desire for greater explanatory power in the analysis stage of the research project. The surveyor may regret, for example, grouping continuous data (data that continues along a spectrum such as age) into discrete categories. What was originally thought would be natural "breaks" in the age categories may not accurately reflect reality. For example, opinions about contemporary worship style may be more striking between people ages twenty-one and twenty-two— when many young people graduate from college and begin their professional careers—than between people ages twenty-nine and thirty. Our counsel is to create categories for response if the question is sensitive (as in level of income) but avoid them for continuous data when possible.

12. Make certain that answer categories do not overlap. A common mistake in questionnaire design is setting up income categories in this way:

    a. Under $10,000
    b. $10,000–$15,000
    c. $15,000–$25,000
    d. $25,000–$40,000
    e. Over $40,000

In this set of answers, someone with an income of $25,000 could choose either of two categories, which reduces the accuracy of this question. The best way to eliminate this problem is by using terms such as *under* and *over* for response categories. For instance, category "b" could be rephrased to increase its accuracy by stating "$15,000–under $25,000." Likewise, category "c" could be restated as "$25,000–under $40,000." Using words such as *under* and *over* clarify the responses without making them unduly complicated.

13. State both sides of the issue: use or imply realistic alternatives. Probably the most difficult question to frame is one that gives the respondent several alternatives. It is difficult to find mutually exclusive alternatives or to provide enough to cover an entire range of options. Also be careful not to word alternatives in such a way that it makes one alternative appear better than the others.

14. **Avoid "yes" and "no" answers.** In many cases, two alternatives cannot adequately measure the range of opinion on a subject. In addition, people have a marked tendency to answer "yes" to yes-or-no questions. Instead of asking, "Are you satisfied with your church?" ask "How satisfied are you with your church: very satisfied, fairly satisfied, not too satisfied, or not at all satisfied?" This makes it easier for respondents to answer and measures gradation of opinion. You may sometimes want to use a scale to measure the intensity of opinion: "With a +5 being the highest ranking and -5 the lowest, how would you rate the following…"

15. **Avoid double negatives.** Often survey questions will use double negatives with a "yes/no" response category that is confusing to the respondent. Consider the following example:

Should the youth program not be directly overseen by the senior pastor?
☐ Yes
☐ No

The following revised version is much clearer for respondents:

Who should oversee the youth program?
☐ The senior pastor
☐ A volunteer youth leader

16. **Do you want to allow neutral ground?** When designing answer categories, whether in words or numbers, there is no fixed rule about whether to allow people to choose from among four (forcing them to choose if they are more positive or more negative), or whether to provide five choices (providing them with neutral ground). Think about how the survey team will use the results and then provide an even or odd number of choices, depending upon those uses.

17. **Place sensitive questions, such as those about age and income, at the end of the questionnaire.** Some people are uncomfortable being asked about their age, income, educational status, and other personal questions. Saving those questions until last increases

DR. GALLUP'S "QUINTAMENSIONAL APPROACH"

Dr. George Gallup pioneered what has been called the "quintamensional approach" to questionnaire design. It probes five aspects of opinion:

1. the respondent's awareness and general knowledge about the topic,
2. the respondent's overall opinions,
3. the reasons the respondent holds these views,
4. the respondent's views on specific aspects of the problem, and
5. the intensity with which the respondent holds these opinions.

the chance of getting answers if the respondent already feels comfortable after answering other questions. It is also helpful to explain that this information is asked for statistical purposes only. This data is useful for several reasons: 1) to describe and understand the characteristics of your congregation, 2) to examine response by background categories such as gender or age, 3) to determine whether those who completed the questionnaire are representative of the sample as a whole. Be careful not to solicit too much personal information, so that you do not inadvertently betray confidentiality.

18. **Use careful "skip logic."** Some questionnaires include questions aimed at a specific group of respondents, such as young people or those who watch religious television, and not at the entire survey population. In such cases, use "filter" or "screener" questions to sort the respondents into appropriate groups. For example, to screen for religious television viewers, ask "Have you watched any religious television programs in the past month?" Those who answer "yes" should also answer the next question, but those who answer "no" should "skip" over the next question to the one that follows. Skip instructions should be prominently displayed alongside the appropriate answer categories. Skip logic can become tricky when using more than one "filter" question. Always have someone check the questionnaire for skip logic before using it.

19. **Use "filter" questions to separate informed from uninformed opinion on complex subjects.** Ask a question like "Have you heard or read about Plan X?" and ask follow-up questions only to those who answer affirmatively. These can serve as guidelines when developing questions that measure one's opinion—whether they deal with the new senior pastor, the building campaign, or the church's ministry to the homeless.

20. **Try not to include many "open-ended" questions.** It is always tempting to ask open-ended questions; that is, instead of including a list of responses from which respondents have to choose, the respondent is asked to explain his or her position. Limit the number of open-ended questions to one or two on the questionnaire. There are two major reasons for this advice:

   ◆ First, including too many of these questions will seriously change the response rate. Answering open-ended questions requires more time and thought than selecting answers from a pre-existing list of alternatives. By including too many open-ended questions, respondents may decide it is too much trouble to complete the questionnaire.

   ◆ Second, including too many open-ended questions will change the mix of people who complete the questionnaire. For example, it discourages those with poor verbal skills and encourages those with more free time.

   Processing the answers for open-ended questions into codes is quite time-consuming. (We explain this process in a later section of the book.)

21. Always include a final open-ended question. The advice we offer above does not apply to the inclusion of a final open-ended question. In any self-administered questionnaire, it is useful to include a final question: "Is there anything you would like to tell us that may not have been covered in this questionnaire?" Anticipate a variety of answers, but this final question compensates for a question in which the alternatives given may not have satisfied a respondent, it allows those who feel the questionnaire "missed the real point" to tell you about it, and it brings to the surface new issues you may want to address at other times in other ways. While you may want to cluster these responses into groups, study them carefully for insights they provide regarding the spectrum of opinions in the congregation.

22. Use boxes in vertical format. For close-ended responses, use boxes that respondents may check instead of providing blanks or having them circle answers. When the check is contained within the box, there is little doubt about which response is marked. The most common format is to place response categories below one another (vertical layout) as opposed to beside one another (horizontal layout). The vertical format distinguishes response categories from the question and from one another, making it easier for the respondent to identify possible answers.

23. Pre-code response categories. When providing categories for response, place numbers in front of the boxes that will mark the respondent's answer. This helps a great deal with coding responses after the interviews are complete. Notice that if the number of responses is ten or greater, the categories should be coded with two digits (example 1). For responses with nine or fewer categories, single digits will suffice (example 2). We will say more about this later, but for now, notice the layout of these examples:

Example 1

01 ☐ three times a day or more
02 ☐ about twice a day
03 ☐ about once a day
04 ☐ several times this week
05 ☐ once this week
06 ☐ about three times this month
07 ☐ about two times this month
08 ☐ about once this month
09 ☐ none
10 ☐ don't know

Example 2

1 ☐ yes
2 ☐ no
3 ☐ don't know

24. Define first. If definitions are necessary for answering the question, provide the definition or any qualifying phrases before the actual question is asked. As always, if providing response categories, these should be stated last. For example, a good structure would be something like, "Next we want to ask you about your attendance at certain voluntary groups in the community. Let's start with church or synagogue. If you exclude special events such as religious holidays like Christmas, Easter, or Passover, or weddings and funerals, about how frequently have you

 Qualifying phrases can make their task of remembering easier.

attended religious services at a local church or synagogue in the past six months? Would you say it is once a week, two or three times a month, once a month, about once or twice in the past six months, or not at all?"

25. Try it out on family and friends. Ask friends and members of your family various questions that are being considered for the survey. Ask them to describe what they think the question is asking and how they arrive at their answer. This is one of the most fruitful ways of learning how questions and response categories are understood by others.

IMPROVING THE QUESTIONNAIRE

One of the best ways to improve survey questions is through the use of qualifiers—clauses or phrases that limit the scope of a question and make the respondent's task easier. Often survey questions require the respondent to remember particular activities (as a rule of thumb, never ask someone to remember their motivations—they typically either cannot remember them or will remember them incorrectly) that occurred months or years ago. Qualifying phrases can make their task of remembering easier. For instance, instead of asking, "On average, how many times do you go to church every year?" try "How many times did you go to church in 2001?" In addition to limiting questions temporally, effective surveyors often limit questions geographically. Instead of

---

HELPING RESPONDENTS REMEMBER

 Many times survey participants are asked information they cannot recall. One of the survey's objectives involves helping respondents remember past events. Here are a few ways to assist them:

1. **Ask multiple questions that involve participant recall. More questions may stimulate associations that will help the respondent remember the item under investigation.**

2. **Ask questions with great time specificity. Instead of asking, "Over the last year, have you attended a worship service of another faith group?" consider posing the question as "Today is July 1, 2002. Think back to January 1, 2002—exactly six months ago today. In that time period, have you been to a worship service of another faith group?"**

3. **Ask a question that is preceded by some introductory phrases. This prepares the respondent for the question and often helps him recall the needed information more accurately.**

asking people, "Do you think there are too many churches?" you might ask, "Do you think there are too many churches in your neighborhood?"

> ✓ **Survey researchers encourage plagiarism when it comes to copying question wordings to allow trend comparisons.**

Survey research firms often will employ the assistance of two or three experts in the field being studied. For church-related surveys, we recommend that the team enlist the assistance of a survey researcher and an expert in the field being studied. For example, if your church is sponsoring a survey for a pastor search committee, the survey team would be wise to seek the counsel of someone familiar with survey research, as well as pastoral placements. This might involve finding a sociologist from a local university and an official from your denomination and asking their opinions of the proposed survey—its scope, specific questions being asked, and categories for response. These experts usually can provide helpful suggestions regarding the questionnaire's language and intent. Recognize, of course, that these experts from different fields will offer varying suggestions. The survey team must analyze the experts' recommendations and create a survey instrument that attends to the experts' most germane suggestions while also remaining vigilant about the survey's length. If the survey team is unable to locate experts in the local community, communication via conference calls and e-mail enables the church to enlist the service of experts from practically anywhere in the country. Denominational bodies and other Christian institutions (seminaries, universities, and foundations) often can assist the survey team in locating the most able experts for outside consultation.

REPLICATION

Unlike other fields, survey researchers encourage plagiarism when it comes to copying question wordings, but it is called "replication." Indeed, the researcher considers it a compliment when peers use his or her questions in their own studies, and for good reason. This is the most important part in creating a reliable, accurate survey instrument. Drawing upon the experience of survey professionals produces several benefits. First, by using the exact same question wording, the survey team does not have to worry if differing results have been caused by the inconsistencies in the wording of questions. Second, reusing questions allows the survey team to compare the opinions of your group with another group for additional insight. In other words, if your survey asks a question that has been asked in a nationwide Gallup poll, you will be able to compare the responses in your survey to the national and regional averages. Finally, reusing questions allows trend comparisons to be drawn over time which can be very helpful for your survey project.

A wording change is justified when one is adapting a question from one denomination to another. For instance, a lay Catholic probably would be confused by a reference to "his synod," just as a Presbyterian might not know how to respond to a question about "her diocese." We encourage you to contact the

national headquarters of your denomination to find
out what research they may have done and can share,
including question wordings. (In return, they probably would be pleased to receive a copy of your local
results to the same questions.) At the end of the next
chapter, we have reproduced many of the demographic questions used in the Gallup Poll to collect information about the characteristics of those they survey.
Use them if they are appropriate; change them if you
need to make adjustments.

RESPONSE CATEGORIES

Many response categories naturally emerge from the language of the question.
When asking someone, "Is your church doing a good job meeting the physical
needs of people in your community?" we naturally expect the answer to be "good"
or "poor." However, a simple good/poor answer may not explore the full range of
opinion on the matter. The survey team may, for instance, decide to ask the question with greater specificity: "How good a job is your church doing in meeting the
physical needs of people in your community—very good, fairly good, not so
good, or not good at all?" Notice that this range of response categories yields a
much better measure of people's opinions, and it is determined by the categories
from which respondents are able to choose in answering the item. For telephone
interviews, the number of response categories should be kept to less than five
since respondents will have a difficult time remembering more than four or five
items. Social scientists debate the efficacy of having a neutral, or middle, category
for response categories. For some survey topics, neutrality is revealing and a helpful category for analysis in the survey's objectives. In other cases, it is more meaningful for respondents to make a choice one way or another. There is no absolute
rule, so solicit input from survey team members and use your best judgment.

In the next chapter, we provide several sample surveys developed by Gallup for
particular congregational studies. You will notice that many questions contain categories for response, and these vary according to the items being measured. The
table on page 64 summarizes common categories for response.

In addition to response categories such as these, surveyors can incorporate
scale ratings (the best ones are typically 1-5) that ask the respondent to evaluate a
statement or topic by providing a numeric answer that corresponds to the intensity with which he or she feels on a particular topic. For example, a survey might
state, "Please rate your opinion of the following statement using a scale of 1 to 5,
with 1 meaning 'strongly agree' and 5 meaning 'strongly disagree.' Financial giving
is a meaningful part of my Christian life."

Strongly Agree   **Strongly Disagree**
1   2   3   4   5

CATEGORY MEASURED	AFFIRMATIVE RESPONSE	RESPONSE	NEGATIVE RESPONSE
OPINION	• strongly agree • moderately agree	• uncertain	• moderately disagree • strongly disagree
	• definitely • probably	• maybe	• probably not • definitely not
ENDORSEMENT	• definitely true • true		• false • definitely false
IMPORTANCE	• extremely important	• fairly important	• not very important • not at all important
	• very important • somewhat important		
VALUE	• extremely valuable • very valuable	• somewhat valuable	• not very valuable • not at all valuable
IMPRESSION	• very positive • somewhat positive	• neither negative nor positive	• somewhat negative • very negative
DEGREE	• more		• less
	• completely • for the most part		• to some degree • not at all
SATISFACTION	• very satisfied • mostly satisfied		• mostly dissatisfied • very dissatisfied
FREQUENCY	• often • several times		• once or twice • never
	• always • usually	• sometimes	• seldom • never
AMOUNT	• a lot • a fair amount		• only a little • not at all
	• a great deal • some		• hardly any • none at all
INTENSITY	• severe	• moderate	• mild
RATING	• excellent	• fair	• bad
	• good		• poor

These scaled categories of response can simplify complex items and, if asked in a sequence, allow the interviewer to cover more questions in less time. If the survey intends to measure opinion using a scale like this, it is often best to place scaled items close to one another on the questionnaire. This allows respondents to use similar frames of reference for multiple items. Additionally, it typically means that the interviewer only has to explain the categories once, instead of repeatedly. Explaining the categories for response several times tends to lengthen the amount of time required for survey completion, which means fewer items can be explored in the survey. Careful planning of the sequence of survey items can alleviate this problem.

PRETESTING

It is important to pretest your questionnaire. It is similar to a dress rehearsal for a major musical production. Pretesting helps the team identify potential problems with a nearly final draft of the questionnaire and provides an opportunity to make revisions before undertaking the major part of the study. The pretest experience should help you answer questions such as these:

◆ How long does it take to complete the interview?

◆ Do the questions cover the target issues?

◆ Do respondents understand the questions?

◆ Are the questions free of ambiguity?

◆ Does the order of the questions appear to affect responses?

◆ Do respondents have the necessary knowledge to answer the questions?

◆ Can respondents understand the alternatives in fixed response questions?

◆ Do the close-ended response categories cover the full range of alternatives?

◆ Do any questions seem biased?

Pretesting can be extremely helpful in determining the response categories for various questionnaire items. If the survey team is uncertain of what categories to provide, ask the question in an open-ended format for the pretest stage and then code the responses into categories. Then use the coded categories as categories of response for the actual survey. For instance, your church may be considering a capital improvement that would involve the construction of a youth center for the congregation's student ministry. Unsure of how much people in the church would be willing to donate toward the project, you might ask the question in an open-ended format for the pretest. Once completed, identify the range of amounts offered in the pretest and then categorize the responses into three or four broad categories. If the pretest involved forty respondents, try to place approximately ten responses in each of the four categories. It is likeliest that the divisions will not be symmetrical (category 1 may represent $1-$499, while category 2 may represent $500-$600), but the aim is to have approximately the same number of observations (responses) in each category. Then use those categories in the final survey. In sum, here's the process:

PRETEST QUESTION:

As you may be aware, First Baptist Church is considering the construction of a new youth center for the church's student ministry. If you were asked to donate money toward this project, approximately how much money would you be willing to donate?

> ☒ Keeping the debriefing meeting on task is important, for it is the primary means by which the survey team will learn how to revise the survey.

RESPONSE CATEGORIES AFTER CODING THE PRETEST:

$0-$499	9 respondents
$500-$599	12 respondents
$600-$749	12 respondents
$750-$1250	7 respondents

QUESTION ON THE FINAL SURVEY:

As you may be aware, First Baptist Church is considering the construction of a new youth center for the church's student ministry. If you were asked to donate money toward this project, approximately how much money would you be willing to donate—less than $500, $500 to $599, $600 to $749, or more than $750?

Pretesting involves conducting the survey with ten to forty respondents, ideally using the same format as the actual survey (telephone, mail, or in-person interview). When using interviewers (for telephone or in-person surveys), the survey team usually convenes a debriefing meeting with the interviewers following the pretest. During this meeting, the survey team should review every part of the survey (introduction, each question, transitions, and conclusion) and determine the following:

1. How hesitant were respondents to participate?
2. What problems did interviewers find with particular words or terms used in the questionnaire? Were certain words or phrases difficult to pronounce?
3. Were certain questions more difficult for respondents to answer?
4. How well did the survey flow? Were there awkward breaks in the survey?
5. What logical errors in the skip patterns can be found?
6. For what items did respondents ask for more clarification or greater specification?

Debriefing meetings, like most church committee gatherings, have the potential of being dominated by one or two outspoken individuals. Likewise, unusual interview experiences can occupy a majority of the discussion but not accurately represent the most pressing issues in re-forming the survey. For instance, an outspoken interviewer who contacted a seminary professor may have an interesting account of the numerous theological challenges the professor offered to the survey's questions and categories of response. However, this should not monopolize the debriefing meeting, because this participant does not represent the typical respondent. Keeping the debriefing meeting on task is important, for it is the primary means by which the survey team will learn how to revise the survey.

You might consider asking interviewers to complete a tally sheet for each question as it was encountered on the pretest. Quantifying different behaviors of respondents and interviewers will provide a more objective measurement of the question's effectiveness. In order to tally these behaviors correctly, the survey team will probably need to involve a third-party observer for each interview since the interviewer will be too busy interviewing to take note of his and the respondent's behavior. Consider the following "score card" to use in the pretest stage.

QUESTION:	1	1B	1C	2	3	3B
NO ERRORS OR CORRECT SKIP (question that was correctly handled or skipped appropriately)						
MINOR CHANGES (question was read with minor changes from the script)						
MAJOR CHANGES (question was read with major changes from the script)						
INTERRUPTION (respondent gave an answer before the question was completely read to him)						
REPEAT QUESTION (interviewer had to repeat the question for the respondent)						
PROBES (interviewer had to probe for an answer)						

BEHAVIOR TALLY FOR SURVEY QUESTIONNAIRE

Based upon what you learn in the pretest stage, redraft the questionnaire as necessary. Test the questionnaire again if several changes were made. Depending upon the form and extent of pretesting employed by the survey team, this stage of the project can last from two weeks to three months.

ORGANIZING THE QUESTIONNAIRE

Five items need to be included in the draft questionnaire: an introduction, questions on the survey topic, demographic questions, transitions between sections, and a conclusion. We have already discussed substantive matters regarding question wording and sequence, but we must not neglect the introduction, conclusion, and internal transitions. These are basic to inducing the respondent's cooperation, in helping the questionnaire flow from one section to another, and in leaving a good impression once the survey is complete. One unintentional consequence of these sections is they may bias the answers or the respondents' willingness to participate in the study. For example, if your church sponsors a survey and in the introduction, the interviewer states, "We are conducting a study of people's religious beliefs in the metropolitan area in preparation for Dr. Billy Graham's upcoming crusade," you may bias the respondent's chance of participating in the survey. Some respondents will want to participate because of their positive impression of Dr. Graham's ministry, while others might choose not to participate because they personally do not like him. Hence, it is important to choose the wording of the introductions and transitions very carefully. Be sensitive to the following:

◆ Adjectives and adverbs that convey positive or negative attributes—for example, "The church has been working *quite hard* at developing a more *effective* children's ministry, and now we would like to hear how *good* a job you think they are doing."

◆ Explicit references to civic, community, or church leaders—for example, "Rev. Cook has proposed a plan to relocate our congregation, but some people in the church oppose this plan. Now, I'd like to ask your thoughts on the matter."

In the introduction, attend to the core questions every potential respondent has: who is calling, what do you want, and how did you get my number? Keep the introduction quite brief and without colorful language. Here's a sample introduction you might use for a telephone survey.

"Good evening, I'm calling from CrossPointe Community Church. My name is Howard, and we are conducting a study of people in the greater Princeton area on their attitudes regarding faith and spirituality. I need to speak to the adult in your household who is eighteen or older and will have the next birthday. Who would that be?"

Once the interviewer is talking to the desired respondent, he or she should restate the organization sponsoring the study, tell why it is important, and assure the respondent that there are no right or wrong answers and that his or her answers will be kept confidential. From the example above, notice that the interviewer mentions the organization before his own name; many refusals come as soon as the respondent

hears the name of an unfamiliar person. By placing the name of the organization first, the survey sounds more legitimate, and it avoids the chitchat many telemarketers practice while trying to establish superficial rapport. We also choose to use the word *study* instead of *survey* because many sales calls are disguised as surveys. *Study* connotes a greater degree of professionalism, which may increase the likelihood of a respondent's participation. By closing the introduction with a question, we make a subtle transition into the question-asking phase of the interview. Research shows that the sooner the respondent starts answering questions, the likelier he or she is to participate, particularly if demographic and contentious questions are placed at the end of the survey.

The careful observer will note that the sample introduction does not mention the amount of time required to complete the survey. It is important, however, to provide a rough estimate of time needed when asked by the respondent. The interviewer should indicate the average interview length but also mention that some interviews are shorter or longer, depending upon the individual respondent. Truthfulness and professionalism are crucial in establishing credibility with the potential respondent and in presenting a positive impression of the church that is sponsoring the study.

When drafting a cover letter for a mail questionnaire or an advance letter for a face-to-face interview, these same principles apply. However, letters are much more easily ignored than an interviewer in person or on the telephone. As a result, the letters must be visually compelling, professional, and brief. The following questions should be addressed in the letter.

1. What topic the study is addressing, who is sponsoring it, and how the results will be used. Convey the importance and excitement of being able to determine accurately, efficiently, and inexpensively vital information on the topic at hand.

2. Why the respondent's participation is crucial and how the respondent was selected.

3. Assurance of confidentiality.

4. A contact phone number the respondent may call if he or she has further questions.

If the survey involves many pages, it might be helpful to address the survey length in the cover letter. You might write, "Although the questionnaire might appear long and time-consuming, it should only take fifteen minutes to complete."

INTERNAL LOGIC

The respondent's decision to participate in the interview occurs in stages, so the surveyor must elicit trust and cooperation early on and continue its development during the early parts of the study. Most refusals to participate occur during the introduction or the first few questions. Consequently, the survey team should choose an opening set of questions that are central to the topic, particularly as it is mentioned in the survey introduction, as well as ones that are easy to answer.

Surveys conventionally open with simple, close-ended questions that obtain quick responses from the participant. Save open-ended and personal questions for later sections of the survey when the interviewer has established rapport and the respondent feels more comfortable with the survey.

The survey team should group questions about related matters into categories. The questionnaire should follow a logical progression of ideas; the sequence of categories is as important as the classification of particular questions. Also, when using a similar scale or set of categorical responses (for example, "very important, somewhat important, not very important, or not at all important"), it is easier for

---

HELPFUL HINTS FOR MAIL QUESTIONNAIRES

1. **Print the questionnaire as a booklet.** Print the questionnaire on tabloid-size sheets of paper (11x17-inch) with the pages folded in half to fit the traditional 8½x11-inch format. Response rates are higher to more professional presentation formats.

2. **Avoid italics, shading, and fonts that use proportional spacing.** Many surveys use ALL CAPS for response categories with traditional capitalization for instructions and questions. Others incorporate **bold** and <u>underlined</u> text for different parts of the survey. There are no absolute rules on these formatting decisions, except that the survey should be consistent (if the answer categories are in ALL CAPS for some questions, they should be in ALL CAPS for all questions).

3. **Do not place questions on the front or back pages.** Instead, use these pages as ways of piquing interest in the survey, giving its purpose and how the respondent can make a difference by participating. The back cover can include the final open-ended question, along with a statement thanking respondents for their participation and a reminder of how they should submit the completed questionnaire to the surveyor.

4. **Identify answer categories with numbers on the left to help with coding the questionnaire once it is returned.**

5. **Place response categories vertically to improve the survey's readability.** Answers that are listed horizontally are sometimes overlooked, and it can be difficult to determine which box corresponds to a particular answer.

6. **Make questions and response categories fit onto the same page.**

7. **Avoid mailing questionnaires close to any holidays and during the entire month of December.** These are times that people are away from home and mail begins to stack up. During such times people are less likely to participate in surveys, regardless of the survey's importance to their lives.

the respondent to answer them together. If the respondent has to work too hard in answering questions, he may tire and end the survey early or may answer questions inaccurately. Transitions between sections can help in the respondent's job by providing him or her with signposts along the journey. The key, however, is to keep these transitions brief; typically, a sentence will suffice.

How long is too long? Questionnaire length is highly correlated with respondent participation. Ideally, telephone interviews should last between ten and fifteen minutes, otherwise the quality of responses can deteriorate. In-person interviews may last thirty minutes to one hour, although most respondents prefer a length closer to the former. For mail questionnaires, length is very important because respondents know from the outset the length of the survey. In many instances, the *appearance* of length can be as crucial an influence as the actual number of pages and questions. Many potential respondents will not participate in a survey with small margins and font size, tight spacing, and many open-ended questions. We recommend that mail questionnaires be no longer than eight pages. If you are going to ask respondents to circle answers instead of check boxes in answering questions, space the categories far apart so that the respondent can circle one answer without touching an adjoining category. One solution is to arrange the categories of response vertically instead of horizontally, although this requires more space on the page. Limit instructions to one or two sentences; brief and simple instructions elicit more response. We suggest using a different font style for questions, response categories, and transitions or section headings to increase the questionnaire's visual appeal. If the survey contains skip patterns (in which a particular answer to a certain question entails skipping to another question), use arrows as visual reminders of the skip instructions.

Let us add one final note regarding open-ended questions on mail surveys. Respondents in mail surveys often use obscure abbreviations and provide ambiguous answers to open-ended questions on mail surveys. These challenges, coupled with the problem of illegible handwriting, can make the coding process extremely difficult for mail questionnaire data analysis. At the same time, open-ended questions provide an opportunity for accurate, verbatim comments, so be sure to include some open-ended questions, but not too many.

SPECIAL ISSUES WITH MAIL QUESTIONNAIRES

Since the mail questionnaire is the primary form of communication between the surveyor and the respondent in this form of data collection, its development merits careful consideration. For the first question, select an

TWO COMMON MISTAKES OF TELEPHONE QUESTIONNAIRES

Ask:

1. Are there any questions that are too long?

2. Are there any questions with too many response categories?

Flagging these two common errors is one of the easiest ways to improve a telephone questionnaire.

item that is easy to answer and is neutral in tone.

SPECIAL ISSUES WITH TELEPHONE QUESTIONNAIRES

Good mail questionnaires do not make good telephone questionnaires. With the former, the stimulus is exclusively visual; with the latter, it is solely oral. A mail questionnaire must be visually attractive to the respondent, which is not a factor in designing a telephone questionnaire. However, a telephone questionnaire must help the interviewer make the transition from one item to the next in maintaining the conversational flow of the interview, which is not part of a self-administered mail survey. Unlike mail questionnaires, the telephone questionnaire often contains response categories that are not specifically mentioned to the respondent during the interview but are available for the interviewer to select if given by the respondent. For example, when Gallup surveys people, we do not typically provide the category "don't know" or "refused to answer" as a possible response choice since some respondents might, out of laziness, immediately select one of these categories instead of thinking through an issue. However, these categories are listed on the interviewer's questionnaire so that he or she can mark them if the respondent chooses either of them instead of the list of responses read by the interviewer. This represents a form of pre-coding that makes data tabulation easier after the survey.

ADVANCE LETTER FOR TELEPHONE SURVEYS

Just as a cover letter accompanying a mail questionnaire is designed to elicit greater response and build rapport with the respondent, a letter sent in advance of a telephone or in-person interview may provide information and create goodwill that increases the respondent's likelihood of participating. Sending an advance letter on church letterhead conveys a measure of professionalism that underscores the importance of the survey project. This has been a successful tactic in generating higher response rates. Consider the following example advance letter.

ADVANCE LETTER

Cross✝Pointe Community Church
Princeton, New Jersey

Office of the Senior Pastor

September 1, 2002

Mr. Brad Eubank
18 Farber Road
Princeton, New Jersey 08542

Dear Mr. Eubank:

Within the next week, someone from our church's survey project team will be calling you to invite you to play a vital role in carrying out the next chapter in our church's history. We want to find out your opinions and attitudes about the state of our congregation and how we ought to move forward in the years ahead.

We are writing in advance of the telephone call to let you know that we will be calling and to ask for your participation in the study. The interview will last approximately fifteen minutes, and we anticipate calling sometime between 7:00 and 9:00 p.m. next week. If we call at an inconvenient time, please ask the interviewer to arrange another time next week that would be more convenient.

We need to hear from every member of the congregation, so let me thank you in advance for your participation in this study. We are in the process of drafting a strategic plan for the church's priorities over the next five years, and the information gathered during this survey project will inform the strategic plan to a large extent.

If you have any questions, please feel free to ask the interviewer directly, or feel free to call me at the church anytime. That number is (609) 910-1000.

Faithfully yours,

Howard McNamara
Senior Pastor

Chapter Four:

Sample This! ⊗

In this chapter, we offer ten sample questionnaires that have been used in various surveys conducted by Gallup. After the ten examples, we have also included a list of demographic questions with the wording and choices exactly as they are asked in Gallup surveys. Not only can they provide a model for designing your own survey, but you may also use these actual questions in your own church's survey. You can either photocopy the pages and reproduce these printed surveys or access them electronically for free download of PDF files at www.grouppublishing.com/gallup/surveys. These questionnaires have been designed for telephone and self-administered (through mail) interviews of American adults over age eighteen. For other survey methods, such as personal interviews, adjustments would need to be made. In a telephone or personal interview, the interviewer would need to introduce himself or herself, state the purpose of the call, and explain the overall intent of the survey. Here is a sample introduction:

"Good evening, I am calling on behalf of First Baptist Church. My name is Brad Witherspoon. We are conducting telephone surveys of people living in our community. We have a series of questions we would like to ask regarding religious beliefs and values. There are no right or wrong answers, and there is no single accepted set of religious beliefs. I need to speak with the adult over age eighteen living in your household who has the next birthday. Who would that be?"

✓ SURVEY 1 (P. 77)

This study sponsored by a congregation could be conducted through in-person or telephone interviews. The topics queried include social and moral values, opinions about organized religion, personal religious beliefs, and spiritual practices (Bible reading, prayer), with several good questions for people not currently affiliated with a local faith community.

⊗ SURVEY 2 (P. 88)

This is an interview script for a telephone questionnaire for a general audience (not necessarily in the church) about moral values, personal problems, community challenges, religious activity, and beliefs about God. This is a very good example of asking questions about religious matters without using church jargon or theologically technical terms.

SURVEY 3 (P. 95)

This questionnaire begins with several open-ended questions, which contradicts some of our earlier advice. This works well for surveys involving small populations, such as lay church leaders being interviewed in a focus group discussion. A survey team might use this example to gather information that does not necessarily have to be coded for further analysis. The questionnaire is obviously designed for a survey of people familiar with a particular congregation, its leadership, and its mission. We designed this questionnaire for a church in the midst of a pastoral search, and it is very helpful for churches experiencing a time of transition.

SURVEY 4 (P. 97)

This self-administered survey that could be distributed in person or through the mail was written for church members who are fairly familiar with fundamental Christian doctrines and spiritual practices of the faith. Using a single scale, respondents rate themselves on thirty key items that differentiated their lives of faith according to beliefs, spiritual disciplines, and personal moral convictions. This spiritual inventory would be extremely useful in determining where individual congregants are excelling in their spiritual walk, as well as areas for further development.

SURVEY 5 (P. 98)

We designed this telephone questionnaire for the United Methodist Church as it was considering how to restructure the organization as well as assess its organizational priorities. Despite its original intent for a very specific purpose, this questionnaire could easily be adapted for a variety of settings. The language is Christ-centered, which means it would be most effective in measuring opinions of people inside the church. The questionnaire assesses attitudes regarding evangelism, mission, strengthening one's faith, elements of a worship service, and goals for the church; attributes of strong ministers/clergy; and opinions about ecclesiastical structure (such as the Annual Conference). The survey concludes with several basic demographic questions (gender, marital status, age, level of education, and employment) and includes two helpful questions to measure the respondent's level of church involvement.

SURVEY 6 (P. 105)

Although this in-person interview questionnaire contains several questions about religious beliefs and spiritual practice, the primary thrust of this survey is evangelism. Through several open-ended questions, the questionnaire seeks to discover the respondent's attitude regarding church programming and goals before exploring particular aspects of mission and evangelism. After beginning with a question about the participant's definition of evangelism, the questionnaire explores his opinions on the topic and measures his or her church's involvement in evangelistic activities. The questionnaire also includes several good questions on small groups and stewardship.

SURVEY 7 (P. 111)

This telephone questionnaire works well for a survey of an entire community, for it explores personal satisfaction and basic religious involvement without being exclusively Christian in orientation. The survey measures personal spirituality, as well as belief in God and opinions about health and spirituality—all of which are of wide public interest and could be helpful in determining the spiritual climate of a local community.

SURVEY 8 (P. 113)

This self-administered questionnaire was originally designed for new members at a local congregation, and it queries respondents on the importance and effectiveness of various church programs. These include Christian education, worship, outreach, youth ministry, and preaching. The survey concludes by asking their opinions on financial giving, personal involvement in church programs, and priorities for the church. Like Survey 5, this questionnaire includes demographic questions including gender, age, family status, level of education, and employment, as well as several questions about church involvement.

SURVEY 9 (P. 125)

This telephone survey is designed to measure the beliefs, attitudes, and practices of a general audience and does not assume an exclusively Christian orientation. The questionnaire design for items 3, 4, and 5 underscores the importance of interviewer training for complex question structure (measuring an activity, then its salience, and finally the age at which the event occurred). The survey measures individuals' response to a catalog of personal problems and crises and then gradually moves to explore matters relating to faith and a relationship with God.

SURVEY 10 (P. 130)

This final Gallup survey represents a compilation of various topics of interest to a church at a time of transition or change. The survey could be effectively used for self-administered or telephone interview forms of data collection, but the combination of both open- and close-ended questions means that many resources would be required for coding a large number of surveys. The questionnaire asks respondents about the profile of an ideal senior pastor as well as the priorities and plans for the local congregation. Questions about personal religious beliefs and rankings of attitudes on matters of faith are also part of this survey.

BONUS DEMOGRAPHIC QUESTIONS (P. 136)

These are a battery of demographic questions that could be added to the end of any of the ten example surveys provided, or they could be adapted for a questionnaire developed by your survey team. Typically, a surveyor asks demographic questions for their explanatory power in cross-tabulation analysis, which will be addressed later in the book. Because these questions have been standardized and are used by a variety of professional surveys—including Gallup polls—we suggest you copy the exact wording of the questions, although their sequence may be modified for your particular survey project.

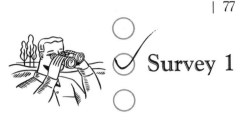 Survey 1

1. How long have you lived in the city or community in which you presently reside?
   - ☐ less than a year
   - ☐ 1-2 years
   - ☐ 3-5 years
   - ☐ 6-9 years
   - ☐ 10-14 years
   - ☐ 15 years or more

2. How active or involved would you say you are in civic, social, and other charitable activities in your neighborhood?
   - ☐ very active
   - ☐ fairly active
   - ☐ only somewhat active
   - ☐ not active at all
   - ☐ haven't lived there that long
   - ☐ don't know
   - ☐ no answer

3. Here are some social changes which might occur in coming years. Would you welcome these or not welcome them?

	Not Welcome	Welcome	No Answer
A. More emphasis on self-expression	☐	☐	☐
B. Less emphasis on money	☐	☐	☐
C. More acceptance of sexual freedom	☐	☐	☐
D. More emphasis on traditional family ties	☐	☐	☐
E. More respect for authority	☐	☐	☐
F. Less emphasis on working hard	☐	☐	☐
G. More acceptance of marijuana usage	☐	☐	☐

4. What is your opinion about a man and a woman having sexual relations before marriage—do you think it is always wrong, almost always wrong, wrong only sometimes, or not wrong at all?
   - ☐ always wrong
   - ☐ almost always wrong
   - ☐ wrong only sometimes
   - ☐ not wrong at all
   - ☐ don't know
   - ☐ no answer

5. What is your religious preference—is it Protestant, Catholic, Jewish, Eastern Orthodox, or some other religion?

☐ Protestant
☐ Catholic
☐ Jewish
☐ Eastern Orthodox
☐ other
☐ none

6. (If answered "Protestant" or "other" to question 5) What specific denomination or faith is that?

_____

7. Now I would like to read you eleven statements. Would you tell me after each whether you strongly agree, moderately agree, are uncertain, moderately disagree, or strongly disagree?

	strongly agree	moderately agree	are uncertain	moderately disagree	strongly disagree	don't know
A. Duty comes before pleasure.	☐	☐	☐	☐	☐	☐
B. An individual should arrive at his or her own religious beliefs independent of any churches or synagogues.	☐	☐	☐	☐	☐	☐
C. Facing my daily tasks is a source of pleasure and satisfaction.	☐	☐	☐	☐	☐	☐
D. Most churches and synagogues today have a clear sense of the real spiritual nature of religion.	☐	☐	☐	☐	☐	☐
E. The rules about morality preached by the churches and synagogues today are too restrictive.	☐	☐	☐	☐	☐	☐
F. Most churches and synagogues today are warm and accepting of outsiders.	☐	☐	☐	☐	☐	☐
G. Most churches and synagogues today are too concerned with organizational, as opposed to theological or spiritual, issues.	☐	☐	☐	☐	☐	☐

	strongly agree	moderately agree	are uncertain	moderately disagree	strongly disagree	don't know
H. Most churches and synagogues today are not concerned with social justice.	☐	☐	☐	☐	☐	☐
I. Most churches and synagogues today are effective in helping people find meaning in life.	☐	☐	☐	☐	☐	☐
J. It doesn't matter what church a person attends—one church is as good as another.	☐	☐	☐	☐	☐	☐
K. I don't have to belong to an organized religion because I live a good life.	☐	☐	☐	☐	☐	☐

8. How important would you say religion is in your own life—would you say it is very important, fairly important, or not very important?
  - ☐ very important
  - ☐ fairly important
  - ☐ not very important
  - ☐ don't know

9. When you were growing up, how important would you say religion was in your own life—would you say it was very important, fairly important, or not very important?
  - ☐ very important
  - ☐ fairly important
  - ☐ not very important
  - ☐ don't know

10. When you were in elementary or grade school, how often did you attend Sunday school or church—every week; two or three times a month; once a month or less; or just on special holidays such as Christmas, Easter, or Yom Kippur?
  - ☐ every week
  - ☐ two or three times a month
  - ☐ once a month or less
  - ☐ only on Christmas, Easter, Yom Kippur, or special holidays
  - ☐ don't know

11. What do you believe about Jesus Christ—do you think Jesus Christ was God or Son of God, another religious leader like Muhammad or Buddha, or never actually lived?
  - ☐ God or Son of God
  - ☐ another leader
  - ☐ never actually lived
  - ☐ don't know

12. Have you ever had a religious experience—that is, a particularly powerful religious insight or awakening?
    - ☐ yes
    - ☐ no
    - ☐ don't know

13. Would you say you have made a commitment to Jesus Christ?
    - ☐ yes
    - ☐ no
    - ☐ don't know

14. Do you believe there is life after death?
    - ☐ yes
    - ☐ no
    - ☐ don't know

15. Do you ever pray to God?
    - ☐ yes
    - ☐ no
    - ☐ don't know

16. Which of the following statements comes closest to describing your feelings about the Bible?
    - ☐ The Bible is the actual Word of God and is to be taken literally, word for word.
    - ☐ The Bible is the inspired Word of God. It contains no errors, but some verses are to be taken symbolically rather than literally.
    - ☐ The Bible is the inspired Word of God, but it may contain historical and scientific errors.
    - ☐ The Bible was not inspired by God, but it represents humankind's best understanding of God's nature.
    - ☐ The Bible is an ancient book of human fables, legends, history, and moral precepts.

17. How many times would you say you prayed privately during the last seven days, not counting mealtimes or church services?
    - ☐ three times a day or more
    - ☐ about twice a day
    - ☐ about once a day
    - ☐ several times this week
    - ☐ once this week
    - ☐ none
    - ☐ don't know

18. Do you think a person can be a good Christian or Jew if he or she doesn't attend church or synagogue?
    - ☐ yes
    - ☐ no
    - ☐ don't know

19. Did you, yourself, happen to receive any religious training as a child?
    - ☐ yes
    - ☐ no
    - ☐ don't know

20. During your youth, did you have confirmation training or special training in preparation for full membership in the church or synagogue?
    - ☐ yes
    - ☐ no
    - ☐ don't know

21. Would you want a child of yours to receive any religious instruction?
    - ☐ yes
    - ☐ no
    - ☐ don't know

22. Are you, yourself, a member of a church or synagogue?
    - ☐ yes
    - ☐ no
    - ☐ don't know

23. Would you invite other persons to join your religious denomination?
    - ☐ yes
    - ☐ no
    - ☐ don't know

24. (If no to question 23) Why wouldn't you invite other persons to join your religious denomination?

25. Have you attended the church or synagogue of your choice in the past **six months,** apart from weddings; funerals; or special holidays such as Christmas, Easter, or Yom Kippur?
    - ☐ yes
    - ☐ no
    - ☐ don't know

26. Have you attended the church or synagogue of your choice within the past **year,** apart from weddings; funerals; or special holidays such as Christmas, Easter, or Yom Kippur?
    - ☐ yes
    - ☐ no
    - ☐ don't know

27. Have you attended the church or synagogue of your choice within the past **two years,** apart from weddings; funerals; or special holidays such as Christmas, Easter, or Yom Kippur?
    - ☐ yes
    - ☐ no
    - ☐ don't know

28. (If yes to question 25) About how many times would you say you attended a church or synagogue in the past **six months**—would you say at least once a week, two or three times a month, or once a month or less?
    - ☐ once a week
    - ☐ two or three times a month
    - ☐ once a month or less
    - ☐ don't know

29. (Ask everyone) Have you seriously considered becoming inactive in the church?
    - ☐ yes
    - ☐ no
    - ☐ don't know

30. Has there ever been a period of **two years or more** when you did not attend church or synagogue, apart from weddings; funerals; or special holidays such as Christmas, Easter, or Yom Kippur?
    - ☐ yes
    - ☐ no
    - ☐ don't know

31. (If yes to question 30) At what age did you stop attending?
    _____

32. (If yes to question 30) When you stopped attending, which of the following statements describe the reasons? (Choose as many as apply.)
    - A. ☐ When I grew up and started making decisions on my own, I stopped going to church.
    - B. ☐ I moved to a different community and never got involved in a new church.
    - C. ☐ I found other interests and activities which led me to spend less and less time on church-related activities.
    - D. ☐ I had specific problems with or objections to the church, its teachings, or its members.
    - E. ☐ The church no longer was a help to me in finding the meaning and purpose of my life.
    - F. ☐ I felt out of place because the church members were more affluent and better educated than I.
    - G. ☐ I felt my lifestyle was no longer compatible with participation in a church.
    - H. ☐ poor health
    - I. ☐ work schedule
    - J. ☐ divorced or separated and did not return to the church
    - K. ☐ another reason

33. (If yes to question 30) Did you begin attending again later?
    - ☐ yes
    - ☐ no
    - ☐ don't know

34. (If yes to question 33) At what age did you begin attending again? _____

35. When you began attending again, what situation or events were most important in your decision to attend? Which of the following statements describe them? (Choose as many as apply.)
    A. ☐ I never attended again.
    B. ☐ I wanted a child of mine to receive religious training.
    C. ☐ I felt an inner need to go back to church.
    D. ☐ I felt an inner need to rediscover my religious faith.
    E. ☐ I was married.
    F. ☐ I was divorced or separated.
    G. ☐ I moved back home.
    H. ☐ I had an important religious experience.
    I. ☐ I couldn't go due to serious illness but was able to return once I got better.
    J. ☐ I was invited to church at an important time.
    K. ☐ I went with my spouse or a relative.
    L. ☐ I got older and thought more about eternal life.
    M. ☐ I felt guilty about not going to church.
    N. ☐ another reason

36. In the past twelve months, has anyone approached you or invited you to become active in a church or synagogue other than your own?
    ☐ yes
    ☐ no
    ☐ don't know

37. (If yes to question 36) Were you approached or invited on more than one occasion?
    ☐ yes
    ☐ no
    ☐ don't know

38. (Note: If response to question 37 is yes, instruct respondent to answer the next four questions in terms of the **most recent** approach or invitation.) By what church or group were you approached? _____

39. Were you approached or invited by someone you know personally such as a relative, friend, or neighbor?
    ☐ yes
    ☐ no
    ☐ don't know

40. Were you approached or invited in person, over the phone, or by an invitation in the mail? (Check all that apply.)
    ☐ personally
    ☐ over the phone
    ☐ by mail
    ☐ other

41. What was your reaction to this approach or invitation—was it favorable or unfavorable?
    - ☐ favorable
    - ☐ unfavorable
    - ☐ don't know

42. In the last two years, did you attend a prayer group, Bible study, or other religious group that meets somewhere other than the church?
    - ☐ yes
    - ☐ no
    - ☐ don't know

43. (If yes to question 42) Did you attend on a regular basis, occasionally, or only once?
    - ☐ on a regular basis
    - ☐ occasionally
    - ☐ only once
    - ☐ don't know

44. In the last two years, have you attended a charismatic religious group; that is, one including the gifts of the spirit?
    - ☐ yes
    - ☐ no
    - ☐ don't know

45. (If yes to question 44) Did you attend on a regular basis, occasionally, or only once?
    - ☐ on a regular basis
    - ☐ occasionally
    - ☐ only once
    - ☐ don't know

46. Have you ever felt unwelcome or excluded from any church because of your race or ethnicity?
    - ☐ yes
    - ☐ no
    - ☐ don't know

47. (If yes to question 46) What church or denomination was that? _____

The following questions should only be asked of those "unchurched" (answered no to question 22 _or_ question 25). Otherwise, this is the end of the interview.

48. In the past, have you been more active or involved in the life of a church or synagogue than you are now?
    - ☐ yes
    - ☐ no
    - ☐ don't know
    - (If yes, continue. If no, thank the respondent for his or her time and end the interview.)

49. How long ago were you last active?
- ☐ less than 1 year ago
- ☐ 1-2 years ago
- ☐ 3-5 years ago
- ☐ 6-10 years ago
- ☐ more than 10 years ago
- ☐ don't know

50. What denomination or faith did you belong to when you were active?
- ☐ Protestant
- ☐ Catholic
- ☐ Jewish
- ☐ Eastern Orthodox
- ☐ other

51. (If answered "Protestant" or "other" to question 50) What specific denomination or faith is that? _____

52. Thinking back to the time when you began to reduce your involvement with the church, can you tell me which of the following statements best describes the reasons? (Choose as many as apply.)
- A. ☐ When I grew up and started making decisions on my own, I stopped going to church.
- B. ☐ I moved to a different community and never got involved in a new church.
- C. ☐ I found other interests and activities which led me to spend less and less time on church-related activities.
- D. ☐ I had specific problems with or objections to the church, its teachings, or its members.
- E. ☐ The church no longer was a help to me in finding the meaning and purpose of my life.
- F. ☐ I felt out of place because the church members were more affluent and better educated than I.
- G. ☐ I felt my lifestyle was no longer compatible with participation in a church.
- H. ☐ poor health
- I. ☐ work schedule
- J. ☐ divorced or separated and did not return to the church
- K. ☐ another reason

53. Which of these statements best describes why you never reaffiliated with a new church? (Choose as many as apply.)
- A. ☐ There were no churches near my new home that were to my liking.
- B. ☐ I waited for someone to approach me, but no one did.
- C. ☐ There were no churches of my preferred denomination at a convenient distance from my new home.
- D. ☐ Representatives of local churches came to call, and I did not like their presentations.
- E. ☐ Seeking a new church was not a matter of urgency, and I never got around to it.
- F. ☐ I didn't want to get involved in organizations in the new community.
- G. ☐ another reason

54. (If question 52 includes D or E, continue. If not, skip to question 55.) You said that you had problems with the church or that it was not helpful. What were your feelings at that time? (Choose as many as apply.)

    A. ☐ dissatisfaction with the pastor or rabbi
    B. ☐ a personal dispute with some members
    C. ☐ teachings about beliefs were too narrow
    D. ☐ teachings about beliefs were too broad and inclusive
    E. ☐ moral teachings on sex and marriage were too narrow
    F. ☐ moral teachings on sex and marriage were too loose
    G. ☐ a dislike for the traditional form of worship
    H. ☐ a dislike for changes from the traditional form of worship
    I. ☐ a dislike for church or synagogue involvement in social or political issues
    J. ☐ too much concern for money
    K. ☐ a feeling that the church or synagogue wasn't willing to work seriously to change the society
    L. ☐ ineffective or poor preaching
    M. ☐ I no longer believed in a supernatural being or force.
    N. ☐ I wanted deeper spiritual meaning than I found in the church or synagogue.
    O. ☐ No one in the church or synagogue seemed to care about me.
    P. ☐ another problem or objection

55. Now think about your present attitude toward the church. Could there be a situation where you could see yourself becoming a fairly active member of a church or synagogue now? Would you say...

    ☐ definitely yes
    ☐ probably yes
    ☐ possibly yes
    ☐ probably no
    ☐ definitely no
    ☐ don't know (do not read this choice)

56. (If answered "probably no" or "definitely no," skip to the next question.) What kind of circumstances would they be? Do any of the following describe them? (Choose as many as apply)

    A. ☐ A new congregation of my preferred denomination is started in my area.
    B. ☐ I am invited to a church or synagogue by a member, and I like the people.
    C. ☐ I find a church or synagogue with good preaching.
    D. ☐ I find a church or synagogue with a good program of religious education for children and youth.
    E. ☐ I find a church or synagogue that is seriously concerned to work for a better society.
    F. ☐ I find a pastor, rabbi, or church or synagogue friends with whom I can openly discuss my spiritual needs.
    G. ☐ I find a pastor, rabbi, or church or synagogue friends with whom I can openly discuss my religious doubts.

H. ☐ There is a change in my family situation; for example, marriage or separation, the birth of a child, or being widowed.

I. ☐ There is a crisis in my life—such as illness, marital problems, or economic problems—and a church or synagogue demonstrates genuine interest in me.

J. ☐ another circumstance

57. Here are some programs that churches sometimes carry on. Are there any of these in which you or someone in your immediate family might be interested in participating?

A. ☐ day-care center

B. ☐ counseling center

C. ☐ adult study program on the Bible or doctrine

D. ☐ neighborhood Bible study or prayer groups for adults

E. ☐ summer programs for children and youth

F. ☐ church school, either released time or religious school

G. ☐ weekend spiritual retreats

H. ☐ programs specifically for men or for women

I. ☐ youth group

J. ☐ a program for single adults

K. ☐ opportunity for participating in cultural programs (music, drama, art, or creative writing)

L. ☐ sports program or camping program (for example, bowling league)

M. ☐ family-oriented activities such as dinners, picnics, or outings

N. ☐ a program to explore different worship styles and religious experiences

O. ☐ charismatic prayer groups

P. ☐ a place where we could go for emergency needs

Q. ☐ senior citizens' program

R. ☐ a "get to know your community" program for newcomers to town

S. ☐ a program for the divorced

T. ☐ a program for young married couples

U. ☐ involvement in public issues

V. ☐ a program for meeting human needs, such as housing for the elderly

Permission to photocopy this survey granted for local church use. Copyright © George H. Gallup Jr. and D. Michael Lindsay. Published in *The Gallup Guide: Reality Check for 21st Century Churches* by Group Publishing, Inc., P.O. Box 481, Loveland, CO 80539. www.grouppublishing.com

Survey 2

1. First, do you have a set of basic values or beliefs that guide your activities?
   - ☐ yes
   - ☐ no
   - ☐ don't know*
   - ☐ no answer*

   *Note: These choices not read to the respondent during any part of the interview, but it is part of the interview script in case the respondent refuses to answer this question.

2. Which of the following is the main source of your present values and beliefs?
   - ☐ what you learned as a child
   - ☐ your own personal experience
   - ☐ the influence of your friends and co-workers
   - ☐ don't know
   - ☐ no answer

3. What is your most basic value or belief?

4. Would you say that your basic understanding of what life is all about has...
   - ☐ changed a lot during the past 5 years
   - ☐ changed a little during the past 5 years
   - ☐ stayed about the same during the past 5 years
   - ☐ don't know
   - ☐ no answer

5. When things are really difficult at work, with your family, or in your personal life, do each of the following help you a great deal, a fair amount, only a little, or not at all?

The thought that...	a great deal	a fair amount	only a little	not at all	don't know	no answer
A. Tough times are just the devil's way of tempting me.	☐	☐	☐	☐	☐	☐
B. Others may be having times that are even tougher.	☐	☐	☐	☐	☐	☐
C. People are depending on me.	☐	☐	☐	☐	☐	☐
D. Other people will still respect me.	☐	☐	☐	☐	☐	☐
E. These times make one a better person.	☐	☐	☐	☐	☐	☐

	a great deal	a fair amount	only a little	not at all	don't know	no answer
F. God will forgive me when I fail.	☐	☐	☐	☐	☐	☐
G. Whoever is responsible for these problems is going to have to pay.	☐	☐	☐	☐	☐	☐
H. I will be rewarded for this difficult time.	☐	☐	☐	☐	☐	☐
I. To accomplish your goal, some difficulty is expected.	☐	☐	☐	☐	☐	☐
J. God is my friend and is always beside me.	☐	☐	☐	☐	☐	☐
K. I'm still the one in charge of situations like these.	☐	☐	☐	☐	☐	☐
L. The situation itself isn't as important as my thoughts and feelings about it.	☐	☐	☐	☐	☐	☐
M. Getting back at those responsible.	☐	☐	☐	☐	☐	☐
N. My religious community understands me when I fail.	☐	☐	☐	☐	☐	☐
O. If only I did what I thought was right, things would be better.	☐	☐	☐	☐	☐	☐
P. Everyone has trouble at some time or another.	☐	☐	☐	☐	☐	☐
Q. I've been through times like this before, and I can make it this time, too.	☐	☐	☐	☐	☐	☐
R. Things will be better soon.	☐	☐	☐	☐	☐	☐
S. It's good to be shaken out of my "rut" and forced to think more deeply about life.	☐	☐	☐	☐	☐	☐
T. I can trust completely in God's grace.	☐	☐	☐	☐	☐	☐
U. God will make things better if I obey.	☐	☐	☐	☐	☐	☐
V. Little things really don't matter that much in the larger scheme of things.	☐	☐	☐	☐	☐	☐

	a great deal	a fair amount	only a little	not at all	don't know	no answer
W. Difficulties aren't so bad if I am really trying to be sensitive to the needs of others.	☐	☐	☐	☐	☐	☐
X. Nothing would ever get done if people gave up whenever things were rough.	☐	☐	☐	☐	☐	☐
Y. Lots of things have been written or said that can help me through times like this.	☐	☐	☐	☐	☐	☐
Z. Having had many different experiences really helps me in times like these.	☐	☐	☐	☐	☐	☐
AA. One has to keep going or suffer the consequences.	☐	☐	☐	☐	☐	☐
BB. I'm trying to do what's right.	☐	☐	☐	☐	☐	☐
CC. Life is a journey, and we learn something more about it every day.	☐	☐	☐	☐	☐	☐

6. On a five-point scale, where "1" means no faith and "5" means a great deal of faith, how would you rate your own faith?

No faith 1 2 3 4 5 Great deal of faith

7. Do you strongly agree, somewhat agree, somewhat disagree, or strongly disagree with each of the following statements?

	strongly agree	somewhat agree	somewhat disagree	strongly disagree	don't know	no answer
A. When everything is going badly, I still know that my life is worthwhile.	☐	☐	☐	☐	☐	☐
B. Many of the things that happen to me just don't seem to fit together or make much sense.	☐	☐	☐	☐	☐	☐
C. Sometimes I wonder if life is worth living.	☐	☐	☐	☐	☐	☐

	strongly agree	somewhat agree	somewhat disagree	strongly disagree	don't know	no answer
D. Sometimes we don't understand what is happening, but we can be sure everything will work out.	☐	☐	☐	☐	☐	☐
E. I think that everything that happens has a purpose.	☐	☐	☐	☐	☐	☐
F. I am not sure what I believe.	☐	☐	☐	☐	☐	☐
G. Religion often hampers humanity's development by making people dependent upon a higher power.	☐	☐	☐	☐	☐	☐
H. A thinking religious person will have doubts about the existence of God.	☐	☐	☐	☐	☐	☐
I. It's best to follow your conscience, regardless of the law.	☐	☐	☐	☐	☐	☐
J. When faced with a tragic event, I try to remember that God still loves me and that there is hope for the future.	☐	☐	☐	☐	☐	☐
K. The best way to live is to take the daily problems as they come and not worry too much about the big questions of life and death.	☐	☐	☐	☐	☐	☐

8. During the last twelve months, have you done any of the following? (Read list)

	yes	no	don't know	no answer
A. Donated money to a charitable cause	☐	☐	☐	☐
B. Given money to religious organizations	☐	☐	☐	☐
C. Given a donation to be used for relief programs, such as famine relief	☐	☐	☐	☐
D. Written letters to a political official or signed a political petition	☐	☐	☐	☐
E. Donated time to helping the poor, disadvantaged, and needy people	☐	☐	☐	☐
F. Donated time to religious work	☐	☐	☐	☐

	yes	no	don't know	no answer
G. Taken part in any group that discusses the values and practices in life	☐	☐	☐	☐
H. Prayed at times of special need	☐	☐	☐	☐
I. Interacted with persons who challenged your basic values	☐	☐	☐	☐
J. Read anything about basic values in life	☐	☐	☐	☐
K. Taken part in a women's or men's support group	☐	☐	☐	☐

9. What is your opinion of the following statements?

	agree	disagree	don't know	no answer
A. There is no one true religion, but there are basic truths and meanings to be found in all the great religions of the world.	☐	☐	☐	☐
B. There is only one true religion.	☐	☐	☐	☐
C. None of the great religions has any truth to offer.	☐	☐	☐	☐

10. How often do you spend quiet moments reflecting on the meaning of life?
    ☐ every day
    ☐ several times a week
    ☐ about once a week
    ☐ several times a month
    ☐ once a month or less
    ☐ never
    ☐ don't know
    ☐ no answer

11. Do you ever pray to God?
    ☐ yes
    ☐ no
    ☐ don't know
    ☐ no answer

12. (If yes to question 11) About how many times would you say you prayed during the last seven days?
    ☐ three times a day or more
    ☐ about twice a day
    ☐ about once a day
    ☐ less than once a day
    ☐ two or three times a week
    ☐ about once a week
    ☐ two or three times a month
    ☐ about once a month
    ☐ other
    ☐ don't know
    ☐ no answer

13. How often do you attend religious services? (Read list)
    - ☐ more than once a week
    - ☐ once a week
    - ☐ two or three times a month
    - ☐ once a month or less
    - ☐ just on special holidays
    - ☐ not at all
    - ☐ don't know
    - ☐ no answer

14. How close does each of the following statements come to your own views about God: very close, somewhat close, not very close, or not close at all?

	very close	somewhat close	not very close	not at all close	don't know	no answer
A. God may exist, but there is no way we can know this.	☐	☐	☐	☐	☐	☐
B. God does not exist.	☐	☐	☐	☐	☐	☐
C. God hears me when I pray.	☐	☐	☐	☐	☐	☐
D. I am uncomfortable about the word *God,* but I do believe in something "more" or "beyond."	☐	☐	☐	☐	☐	☐
E. Jesus is the divine Son of God, and I have no question about it.	☐	☐	☐	☐	☐	☐
F. God inspired our ancestors with a code of ethics by which we live.	☐	☐	☐	☐	☐	☐
G. God gave to Moses basic laws that we should live by.	☐	☐	☐	☐	☐	☐
H. God saves the souls of sinners who believe in Jesus Christ.	☐	☐	☐	☐	☐	☐
I. God is a concept of humankind but does not necessarily exist.	☐	☐	☐	☐	☐	☐

15. Some people have very traditional values about such matters as sex, morality, family life, and religion. On a scale of one to seven where "1" represents someone who has very traditional, conservative values about these matters and "7" represents someone who has very nontraditional, liberal values about these matters, where on this scale would you place yourself? Again, "1" represents very traditional, conservative values, and "7" represents very liberal, nontraditional values. You may, of course, use any number between one and seven. Where on this scale would you place yourself?

1	2	3	4	5	6	7
☐	☐	☐	☐	☐	☐	☐

Permission to photocopy this survey granted for local church use. Copyright © George H. Gallup Jr. and D. Michael Lindsay. Published in *The Gallup Guide: Reality Check for 21st Century Churches* by Group Publishing, Inc., P.O. Box 481, Loveland, CO 80539. www.grouppublishing.com

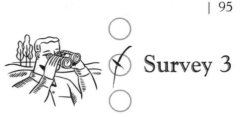

Survey 3

Please feel free to give full answers to the following:

1. Who are we as a church?

2. What are we like as a community?

3. What is God doing in our midst today?

4. What does God want our church to be today?

5. What does God want our church to be in five years?

6. What words would you use to describe our church today?

7. What words would you use to describe what our church can be in five years?

8. Which of these words comes closest to describing **our church?**
- ☐ traditional
- ☐ gospel-centered
- ☐ liturgical
- ☐ rooted in Scripture
- ☐ conservative
- ☐ liberal
- ☐ Orthodox
- ☐ evangelical
- ☐ charismatic
- ☐ other: _____

9. Which of these words comes closest to describing the **ideal pastor?**
- ☐ traditional
- ☐ gospel-centered
- ☐ liturgical
- ☐ rooted in Scripture
- ☐ conservative
- ☐ liberal
- ☐ Orthodox
- ☐ evangelical
- ☐ charismatic
- ☐ other: _____

10. Which of these words comes closest to describing **yourself?**
- ☐ traditional
- ☐ gospel-centered
- ☐ liturgical
- ☐ rooted in Scripture
- ☐ conservative
- ☐ liberal
- ☐ Orthodox
- ☐ evangelical
- ☐ charismatic
- ☐ other: _____

Permission to photocopy this survey granted for local church use. Copyright © George H. Gallup Jr. and D. Michael Lindsay. Published in *The Gallup Guide: Reality Check for 21st Century Churches* by Group Publishing, Inc., P.O. Box 481, Loveland, CO 80539. www.grouppublishing.com

Survey 4

For each of the following statements, please tell me where you would place yourself on a scale from zero to five where "0" stands for "does not apply at all" and "5" stands for "applies completely."

(0 - 5)

___ A. I exist to know, love, and serve God.

___ B. I believe that the God of the Bible is one in essence but distinct in persons—Father, Son, and Holy Spirit.

___ C. I believe that nothing I have done or do can earn my salvation.

___ D. I believe that the Bible has decisive authority over what I say and do.

___ E. I believe that God is actively involved in my life.

___ F. I thank God daily for who God is and what God is doing in my life.

___ G. I desire Jesus Christ to be first in my life.

___ H. I regularly study the Bible to find direction for my life.

___ I. I seek to grow closer to God by listening to God in prayer.

___ J. I am willing to risk everything that is important in my life for Jesus Christ.

___ K. I have inner contentment even when things go wrong.

___ L. I take unpopular stands when my faith dictates.

___ M. I control my tongue.

___ N. I have an inner peace from God.

___ O. No task is too menial for me if God calls me to do it.

___ P. God calls me to be involved in the lives of the poor and suffering.

___ Q. I believe it is important to share my faith with my neighbor because Christ has commanded me to do so.

___ R. I believe that a Christian should live a sacrificial life not driven by pursuit of material things.

___ S. I believe that the community of true believers is Christ's body on earth.

___ T. I believe that all people are loved by God, and, therefore, I should love them.

___ U. I am living out God's purpose for my life.

___ V. I allow other Christians to hold me accountable for my actions.

___ W. I give away my time to serve and help others in my community.

___ X. My first priority in spending is to support God's work.

___ Y. I pray for non-Christians to accept Jesus Christ as their Lord and Savior.

___ Z. God's grace enables me to forgive people who have hurt me.

___ AA. I am known for not raising my voice.

___ BB. I keep my composure even when people or circumstances irritate me.

___ CC. I would never keep money that did not belong to me.

___ DD. I am known as a person who speaks words of kindness to those in need of encouragement.

Permission to photocopy this survey granted for local church use. Copyright © George H. Gallup Jr. and D. Michael Lindsay. Published in *The Gallup Guide: Reality Check for 21st Century Churches* by Group Publishing, Inc., P.O. Box 481, Loveland, CO 80539. www.grouppublishing.com

Survey 5

Please check your answer to each question. Unless stated otherwise, choose only one answer per question.

1. How important is the Christian faith in your life?
   - ☐ extremely important
   - ☐ very important
   - ☐ somewhat important
   - ☐ not at all important

2. Please rate your opinions using the following scale (one to five). Write the number that corresponds to your opinion beside each statement. Please use only whole numbers.

strongly agree				**strongly disagree**
1	2	3	4	5

   ___ Financial giving is a meaningful part of my Christian life.
   ___ I try to bring others to Christ through the way I live or through discussion or through prayer.
   ___ I wish my religious beliefs were stronger.
   ___ My religious faith is the most important influence in my life.

3. Have you personally ever tried to encourage someone to believe in Jesus Christ or accept him as personal Savior?
   - ☐ yes, several times
   - ☐ yes, a few times
   - ☐ no

4. If your answer is "yes" to number 3, when have you done this?
   - ☐ within the past year
   - ☐ 1-5 years ago
   - ☐ 6-10 years ago
   - ☐ more than 10 years ago

5. Please rate your likelihood to participate in these activities using the following scale. (Please circle a response for each item.)

A. Invite a neighbor to attend your church.	**very likely**	**somewhat likely**	**not at all likely**
B. Invite a co-worker to attend your church.	**very likely**	**somewhat likely**	**not at all likely**
C. Visit inactive members.	**very likely**	**somewhat likely**	**not at all likely**
D. Canvas nearby neighborhoods for prospective members.	**very likely**	**somewhat likely**	**not at all likely**

6. Please check the response that most closely matches your opinion of the following statements:

I am well equipped to talk about my faith in Jesus Christ with others.
- ☐ agree strongly
- ☐ agree somewhat
- ☐ disagree somewhat
- ☐ disagree strongly

I am comfortable sharing my faith with...

A. family
- ☐ very comfortable
- ☐ somewhat comfortable
- ☐ not at all comfortable

B. friends
- ☐ very comfortable
- ☐ somewhat comfortable
- ☐ not at all comfortable

C. co-workers
- ☐ very comfortable
- ☐ somewhat comfortable
- ☐ not at all comfortable

D. strangers
- ☐ very comfortable
- ☐ somewhat comfortable
- ☐ not at all comfortable

7. For your local congregation as it stands now, which statement do you believe best describes your church's work in missions? Please check one answer per statement.

A. In local missions (within a thirty-mile radius), would you say your church is...
- ☐ very supportive
- ☐ fairly supportive
- ☐ not at all supportive

B. In North American missions (not local), would you say your church is...
- ☐ very supportive
- ☐ fairly supportive
- ☐ not at all supportive

C. In overseas missions, would you say your church is...
- ☐ very supportive
- ☐ fairly supportive
- ☐ not at all supportive

8. How would you rate your church in terms of preparing and/or training you to share Christ with others?
- ☐ excellent
- ☐ good
- ☐ fair
- ☐ poor

9. What of the following, if any, do you do to nourish or strengthen your faith or sense of meaning in life? (Please check all that apply.)

☐ pray or meditate alone
☐ attend religious services
☐ study the Bible or religious topics in a church
☐ attend a class or study group
☐ discuss personal problems with a pastor or other religious counselor
☐ read the Bible or other religious books
☐ participate in small group prayer and/or Bible study
☐ other: (please specify) _____
☐ none

10. In what area do you desire the greatest help in strengthening your faith? (Please check only one answer.)

☐ pray or meditate alone
☐ attend religious services
☐ study the Bible or religious topics in a church
☐ attend a class or study group
☐ discuss personal problems with a pastor or other religious counselor
☐ read the Bible or other religious books
☐ participate in small group prayer and/or Bible study
☐ other: (please specify) _____
☐ none

11. Which of the following most assists you in experiencing God's presence in your life? (Please check only one answer.)

☐ Sunday worship
☐ meaningful relationships with other Christians
☐ hearing stories of God's work in the world
☐ personal times of reflection
☐ reading the Bible
☐ sharing in a small group
☐ witnessing to others
☐ other: _____

12. From your point of view, how would you rate the following in importance for meaningful worship? (Please circle a response for each item.)

A. hymns/choruses	extremely important	very important	somewhat important	not at all important
B. choir music/special music	extremely important	very important	somewhat important	not at all important
C. corporate prayer	extremely important	very important	somewhat important	not at all important
D. individual prayer	extremely important	very important	somewhat important	not at all important
E. sermon	extremely important	very important	somewhat important	not at all important
F. testimony	extremely important	very important	somewhat important	not at all important
G. multimedia/video/drama	extremely important	very important	somewhat important	not at all important

13. Which of the following do you consider to be the three most important goals for a vital, growing church? (Please check three items.)

___ A. to increase awareness of pressing social issues
___ B. to deepen prayer life
___ C. to encourage a stronger commitment to Jesus Christ
___ D. to increase knowledge of the traditions and policy of the church
___ E. to increase biblical knowledge
___ F. to raise the level of financial giving
___ G. to deepen the understanding of stewardship
___ H. to better equip people for evangelism
___ I. to increase social outreach to the community
___ J. to bring about more unity within the church
___ K. other: _____

14. Which of the following statements best describes why nonmembers do not affiliate with a church? (Please check only one answer.)

☐ There are no churches of their preferred denomination within a convenient distance from their homes.
☐ None of the churches near their homes are to their liking.
☐ No one approached them about affiliating with a local church.
☐ Someone from a church approached them, but they did not like the person who visited them or the manner in which the person visited them.
☐ People pursue other interests and activities and do not have time for church.
☐ They have specific problems or objections to the church, its teachings, or its leadership.
☐ The church is not perceived as helpful in finding meaning and purpose for their lives.
☐ People move to a new community and never get involved in a new church.
☐ There is no urgent reason for affiliating, and they simply have not gotten around to doing it.
☐ other: _____

15. How would you rate the following in the life of your congregation? (Please circle a response for each item.)

A. evangelism	extremely important	very important	somewhat important	not at all important
B. outreach to the poor	extremely important	very important	somewhat important	not at all important
C. tithing/giving	extremely important	very important	somewhat important	not at all important
D. level of church attendance	extremely important	very important	somewhat important	not at all important
E. spiritual nourishment	extremely important	very important	somewhat important	not at all important
F. sense of community	extremely important	very important	somewhat important	not at all important
G. small group involvement	extremely important	very important	somewhat important	not at all important

16. What, in your view, is the most important leadership quality that members of the clergy need in order to face the challenges of the 21st century?
- ☐ strong interpersonal/pastoral care skills
- ☐ educated and knowledgeable
- ☐ effective speaker and teacher
- ☐ dynamic personality/inspirational
- ☐ strong administrative skills
- ☐ creative/innovative leader
- ☐ effective with evangelism
- ☐ interested in matters of social justice
- ☐ ability to deal with change

17. Which TWO of the following societal problems do you feel most need the attention of the United Methodist Church? (Please check two items.)
- ☐ problems of minority groups
- ☐ intolerance
- ☐ inner-city problems
- ☐ divorced, separated families
- ☐ racism
- ☐ abortion
- ☐ poverty
- ☐ hunger
- ☐ homelessness
- ☐ AIDS
- ☐ inadequate education
- ☐ homosexuality as it relates to the church
- ☐ alcohol and drug addiction

18. How much of your income, if any, do you give to your church?
- ☐ 1-5 %
- ☐ 6-9 %
- ☐ 10-15 %
- ☐ more than 15%
- ☐ none at all

19. By your definition, how often do you tithe?
- ☐ always
- ☐ usually
- ☐ sometimes
- ☐ seldom
- ☐ never

20. Do you plan to tithe in the future?
- ☐ definitely
- ☐ probably
- ☐ maybe
- ☐ probably not
- ☐ definitely not

21. Have you heard or read about the United Methodist Annual Conference?
- ☐ yes
- ☐ no

22. Our annual conference provides resources and training for local churches. In which of the following topics, in your opinion, should our annual conference provide resources and training for local churches?
- ☐ dealing with conflict
- ☐ planning for ministry
- ☐ stewardship
- ☐ nurture
- ☐ outreach
- ☐ witness
- ☐ ministry with children
- ☐ ministry with the poor
- ☐ dealing with change
- ☐ spiritual growth
- ☐ leadership skills
- ☐ other: _____

The following section is for demographic purposes only, and like the rest of the survey, is anonymous.

23. Are you...
- ☐ male
- ☐ female

24. What is your marital status?
- ☐ single, never married
- ☐ married
- ☐ separated
- ☐ divorced
- ☐ widowed

25. What is your age?
- ☐ 18-29 years
- ☐ 30-49 years
- ☐ 50-64 years
- ☐ 65 and over

26. What is your level of education?
- ☐ some high school
- ☐ high school graduate
- ☐ technical/trade school
- ☐ some college
- ☐ college graduate
- ☐ some postgraduate work
- ☐ master's/professional degree
- ☐ doctoral degree

27. What is your current employment status?
- ☐ full time
- ☐ part time
- ☐ student
- ☐ homemaker
- ☐ unemployed
- ☐ retired
- ☐ other: _____

28. How actively involved would you say you are in your church and in church activities?
- ☐ a great deal
- ☐ somewhat
- ☐ not much
- ☐ hardly at all

29. Do you presently hold a leadership position or role in your church?
- ☐ yes
- ☐ no

Permission to photocopy this survey granted for local church use. Copyright © George H. Gallup Jr. and D. Michael Lindsay. Published in *The Gallup Guide: Reality Check for 21st Century Churches* by Group Publishing, Inc., P.O. Box 481, Loveland, CO 80539. www.grouppublishing.com

Survey 6

I. Overall Views About Church

1. What, in your opinion, is the biggest challenge facing your local church at the present time?

2. In what ways, if any, has your local church changed over the last five years?

3. And in what ways, if any, would you like to see it change during the next five years?

4. What new programs or activities would you like to see developed or strengthened?

II. Plans for Your Church

5. What long-term goals, if any, do you have for your church in programs and ministry?

6. Which of the following do you consider to be the three most important goals for your church and parishioners?
   - ☐ to deepen prayer life
   - ☐ to increase knowledge of the traditions of the church
   - ☐ to increase biblical knowledge
   - ☐ to increase awareness of pressing social issues
   - ☐ to better equip people for evangelism
   - ☐ to deepen the understanding of stewardship
   - ☐ to raise the level of financial giving
   - ☐ to bring about more unity within your church
   - ☐ to encourage a stronger commitment to Jesus Christ
   - ☐ to increase social outreach to the community

7. Does your church happen to have a specific long-term plan of action?
- ☐ yes
- ☐ no

8. Does the lay leadership of your church share your vision for the church?
- ☐ completely
- ☐ for the most part
- ☐ to some degree
- ☐ not at all
- ☐ don't know

III. Programs in Church

9. Which of these programs or activities do you currently have in your church? Which would you like to develop?

	currently have	like to develop
A. support groups	☐	☐
B. adult Bible study groups	☐	☐
C. youth program	☐	☐
D. evangelism training	☐	☐
E. weekend retreats	☐	☐
F. social events	☐	☐
G. prayer meetings	☐	☐
H. social outreach programs	☐	☐

IV. Definition of Evangelism

10. What is your own understanding of evangelism?

11. Which of the following do you regard as important ways to carry out or stimulate evangelism?
- ☐ "Lifestyle Evangelism"—living in such a way as to bring others to Christ
- ☐ persuading others to accept your beliefs
- ☐ mutual sharing of life stories
- ☐ apologetics
- ☐ Bible study and teaching
- ☐ prayer and sharing groups
- ☐ invitation by parishioners to attend church with them
- ☐ meeting the needs of the disadvantaged
- ☐ sermons

V. Importance of Evangelism

12. Do you agree or disagree with this statement: Evangelism is the presentation of Jesus Christ, in the power of the Holy Spirit, in such ways that persons may be led to believe in him as Savior and follow him as Lord within the fellowship of the church.
    - ☐ agree completely
    - ☐ agree somewhat
    - ☐ disagree somewhat
    - ☐ disagree completely
    - ☐ no opinion

13. Do you think evangelism is a vital part of Christian commitment?
    - ☐ yes
    - ☐ no

14. In what evangelistic ways, if any, are you presently involved?

15. Does your church have any plans to encourage evangelism among the parishioners in the next decade?
    - ☐ yes
    - ☐ no

16. To what extent, if any at all, do you think the members of your church are prepared for evangelism?
    - ☐ very well prepared
    - ☐ fairly well prepared
    - ☐ not at all prepared
    - ☐ don't know

17. How important do you think it is for members of your church to participate in evangelism?
    - ☐ very important
    - ☐ fairly important
    - ☐ not important
    - ☐ no opinion

18. What evangelistic activities have you found to be most effective?

VI. Your Own Beliefs

19. How would you best express your understanding of the gospel?

20. Do you feel comfortable talking about Jesus Christ with members of your church?
    ☐ yes
    ☐ no

21. Do you ever have occasion to share your own personal testimony with people in your church?
    ☐ yes
    ☐ no

22. Do you happen to participate in any small group of Bible study or prayer within your church?
    ☐ yes
    ☐ no

23. Do you happen to set aside time each day for personal devotions?
    ☐ yes
    ☐ no

24. Do you happen to set aside time each day for prayer or meditation?
    ☐ yes
    ☐ no

25. Which one of these statements comes closest to describing your beliefs about Jesus?
    ☐ Jesus was divine in the sense that he was in fact God living among people.
    ☐ Jesus was divine in the sense that while he was only a person, he was uniquely called by God to reveal God's purpose in the world.
    ☐ Jesus was divine in that he embodied the best that is in all people.
    ☐ Jesus was a great man and teacher, but I would not call him divine.
    ☐ other: _____

26. To what extent do you believe that Jesus Christ is the incarnate Son of God and that he has done everything necessary for our salvation?
    ☐ believe completely
    ☐ believe for the most part
    ☐ do not believe

27. Do you believe in the physical or bodily resurrection of Jesus Christ?
    ☐ yes
    ☐ no

VII. Small Groups

28. Do you happen to have small groups in your church that meet for prayer, sharing, and Bible study?
    ☐ yes
    ☐ no

29. (If yes to question 28) It has been said that small groups that meet in Christ's name are helpful for building the church and preparing the laity for evangelism and mission. Do you agree or disagree?
   - ☐ agree
   - ☐ disagree
   - ☐ no opinion

30. Do you think these groups are an effective evangelistic tool, in terms of equipping people for evangelism?
   - ☐ yes
   - ☐ no
   - ☐ no opinion

31. Do you, yourself, happen to be involved in such a group, either as a leader or a participant?
   - ☐ yes, as a leader
   - ☐ yes, as a participant
   - ☐ no

32. (If no to question 28) Are you interested in getting such small groups started in your church?
   - ☐ yes
   - ☐ no

33. Would you, yourself, be interested in participating in such a group?
   - ☐ yes
   - ☐ no

VIII. Stewardship

34. Are there any special efforts in your church to inform members about the full meaning of stewardship (not just the financial aspect)?
   - ☐ yes
   - ☐ no

35. Are your stewardship efforts pretty much limited to a specified period of time, or is it year-round?
   - ☐ specific period of time
   - ☐ year-round

IX. Missionary Activity

36. Does your church support any missionary efforts?
   - ☐ yes
   - ☐ no

37. Does your church happen to sponsor individual people or couples who are missionaries or who intend to be?
   - ☐ yes
   - ☐ no

38. In your view, how important are missions and missionary activity?
- ☐ very important
- ☐ fairly important
- ☐ not at all important

X. Sharing Faith

39. Does your church have a program that trains people to be able to share their faith with others?
- ☐ yes
- ☐ no

40. In your church are people given the opportunity to talk about their spiritual journeys?
- ☐ yes
- ☐ no

41. How important is it to you that you have a sense of where people are in their spiritual journeys?
- ☐ very important
- ☐ fairly important
- ☐ not very important
- ☐ no opinion

Permission to photocopy this survey granted for local church use. Copyright © George H. Gallup Jr. and D. Michael Lindsay. Published in *The Gallup Guide: Reality Check for 21st Century Churches* by Group Publishing, Inc., P.O. Box 481, Loveland, CO 80539. www.grouppublishing.com

Survey 7

1. In general, how satisfied would you say you are with your life at this time—would you say you are...
- □ very satisfied
- □ mostly satisfied
- □ mostly dissatisfied
- □ very dissatisfied
- □ don't know

2. How important would you say religion is in your own life?
- □ extremely important
- □ very important
- □ fairly important
- □ not too important
- □ not at all important
- □ don't know

3. How frequently do you do each of the following activities—at least once a day, a few times a week, a few times a month, a few times a year, or not at all?

	once a day	a few times a week	a few times a month	a few times a year	not at all	don't know
A. read the Bible or holy Scriptures	□	□	□	□	□	□
B. attend religious or worship services	□	□	□	□	□	□
C. take part in a small prayer group or religious study group	□	□	□	□	□	□
D. join in evangelism, outreach, or mission work	□	□	□	□	□	□
E. pray or meditate by yourself	□	□	□	□	□	□

4. (If prays or meditates at all; that is, gives any response *except* "not at all" or "don't know," ask) Which of these do you do when you pray or meditate by yourself? (Check all that apply.)
- ☐ meditate or try to get in touch with God or your higher power
- ☐ talk with God in your own words
- ☐ read from a book of prayers
- ☐ ask God for material things that you may need including employment and good health
- ☐ sit quietly and just think about God
- ☐ ask God to speak and then wait in silence for God's reply
- ☐ sit quietly and meditate, using an Eastern meditation practice
- ☐ sit quietly and meditate, using a secular meditation practice

5. How often have you felt as though you were very close to or at one with a powerful spiritual presence?
- ☐ often
- ☐ several times
- ☐ once or twice
- ☐ never
- ☐ don't know

6. Do you believe in God or a universal spirit?
- ☐ yes
- ☐ no
- ☐ don't know

7. Which of these statements comes closest to your own opinion? (Read choices)
- ☐ God acts directly through supernatural intervention to heal you or keep you well.
- ☐ The spiritual nature of your thinking and your relationship with God helps you stay healthy and helps heal you if you are not well.
- ☐ God does not usually act at all to heal or maintain good health.
- ☐ You do not believe that there is a God or higher power.

Permission to photocopy this survey granted for local church use. Copyright © George H. Gallup Jr. and D. Michael Lindsay. Published in *The Gallup Guide: Reality Check for 21st Century Churches* by Group Publishing, Inc., P.O. Box 481, Loveland, CO 80539. www.grouppublishing.com

Survey 8

1. Which of the following were factors in your decision to join this church? (Check all that apply.)
   - ☐ nearest church in my denomination
   - ☐ church was good compromise for families with different religious backgrounds
   - ☐ friends/neighbors were members
   - ☐ warm welcome
   - ☐ quality of sermons
   - ☐ style of worship
   - ☐ music program
   - ☐ quality of the Sunday school/youth programs
   - ☐ ministers
   - ☐ church activities/programs
   - ☐ family atmosphere
   - ☐ spiritual atmosphere
   - ☐ where one feels the presence of Jesus Christ
   - ☐ the people/fellowship
   - ☐ other (please list) _____

2. How well do you feel you fit into this church community?
   - ☐ very well
   - ☐ fairly well
   - ☐ not at all well

3. How important to you is it that this church offers the following:

	very important	fairly important	not at all important
A. Sunday school	☐	☐	☐
B. men's/women's Bible study	☐	☐	☐
C. evangelism training	☐	☐	☐
D. support groups	☐	☐	☐
E. fellowships	☐	☐	☐
F. weekend retreats	☐	☐	☐
G. volunteer opportunities to serve	☐	☐	☐
H. children's programs	☐	☐	☐
I. youth programs	☐	☐	☐
J. single adult programs	☐	☐	☐
K. senior adult programs	☐	☐	☐
L. social outreach/missions programs	☐	☐	☐

4. What ministry programs or opportunities are not currently offered that you would like to see included?

5. How important to you, personally, are the following:

	very important	fairly important	not at all important
A. Sunday morning worship	☐	☐	☐
B. Sunday school/adult education	☐	☐	☐
C. Sunday evening worship	☐	☐	☐
D. midweek worship	☐	☐	☐
E. holiday programs/special events	☐	☐	☐
F. choral music during services	☐	☐	☐
G. congregational hymns and singing	☐	☐	☐
H. organ/instrumental music during services	☐	☐	☐
I. general content and delivery of sermons	☐	☐	☐
J. prayer meeting	☐	☐	☐
K. sense of closeness to God in worship	☐	☐	☐
L. warmth and feeling of Christian community	☐	☐	☐
M. evangelism training	☐	☐	☐
N. support groups	☐	☐	☐
O. fellowships	☐	☐	☐
P. weekend retreats	☐	☐	☐
Q. children's programs	☐	☐	☐
R. youth programs	☐	☐	☐
S. single adult programs	☐	☐	☐
T. senior adult programs	☐	☐	☐

6. How good a job is this church doing with each of these?

	excellent	good	only fair	poor
A. Sunday morning worship	☐	☐	☐	☐
B. Sunday school/ adult education	☐	☐	☐	☐
C. Sunday evening worship	☐	☐	☐	☐
D. midweek worship	☐	☐	☐	☐
E. holiday programs/ special events	☐	☐	☐	☐
F. choral music during services	☐	☐	☐	☐
G. congregational hymns and singing	☐	☐	☐	☐
H. organ/instrumental music during services	☐	☐	☐	☐
I. general content and delivery of sermons	☐	☐	☐	☐
J. prayer meeting	☐	☐	☐	☐
K. sense of closeness to God in worship	☐	☐	☐	☐
L. warmth and feeling of Christian community	☐	☐	☐	☐
M. evangelism training	☐	☐	☐	☐
N. support groups	☐	☐	☐	☐
O. fellowships	☐	☐	☐	☐
P. weekend retreats	☐	☐	☐	☐
Q. children's programs	☐	☐	☐	☐
R. youth programs	☐	☐	☐	☐
S. single adult programs	☐	☐	☐	☐
T. senior adult programs	☐	☐	☐	☐

7. What emphasis would you like given to the following areas:

	a great deal	some	hardly any	none
A. homebound visits	☐	☐	☐	☐
B. hospital visits	☐	☐	☐	☐
C. baptismal preparation/ counseling	☐	☐	☐	☐
D. wedding preparation/ counseling	☐	☐	☐	☐
E. marriage counseling and support	☐	☐	☐	☐
F. family concerns				
G. death and dying concerns	☐	☐	☐	☐
H. homelessness/ hunger	☐	☐	☐	☐

	a great deal	some	hardly any	none
I. substance abuse	☐	☐	☐	☐
J. sexuality	☐	☐	☐	☐
K. racial concerns	☐	☐	☐	☐

8. How often do you attend Sunday school/adult education?
   - ☐ weekly
   - ☐ three times a month
   - ☐ one or two times a month
   - ☐ six times a year or less
   - ☐ never

9. If you attend six times a year or less, or never, what are the main reasons? (Check all that apply.)
   - ☐ conflict with other church activity
   - ☐ outside activity conflict
   - ☐ not interested
   - ☐ dissatisfied with content
   - ☐ dissatisfied with presentation
   - ☐ other (please specify) _____

10. What Sunday morning programs would you like to see offered at this church? (Check all that apply.)
    - ☐ large group meetings
    - ☐ small group meetings
    - ☐ pastor's forum
    - ☐ church-wide fellowship
    - ☐ Bible study
    - ☐ sermon dialogue
    - ☐ book reviews
    - ☐ support groups
    - ☐ divorce support groups
    - ☐ parenting support groups
    - ☐ bereavement
    - ☐ general healing for damaged emotions
    - ☐ twelve-step programs

11. Are there programs offered at this church that you wish to attend that you cannot because of when they are scheduled?
    - ☐ yes
    - ☐ no
    - If yes, which ones? _____

12. Which topics would you like to hear addressed in some forum? (Check all that apply.)
- ☐ living a Christian life
- ☐ history of this church's denomination
- ☐ worship and liturgy
- ☐ the church's response to current events and issues
- ☐ theological issues
- ☐ personal faith journeys
- ☐ local community issues
- ☐ music
- ☐ international issues/world peace
- ☐ other topics (please specify): _____

13. If Sunday school/adult education were offered on a weeknight, what would be your preference? (Check all that apply.)
- ☐ Monday
- ☐ Tuesday
- ☐ Wednesday
- ☐ Thursday
- ☐ Friday
- ☐ biweekly
- ☐ could not attend any
- ☐ not interested

14. How welcoming an atmosphere do you feel this church has toward newcomers?
- ☐ excellent
- ☐ good
- ☐ only fair
- ☐ poor
- ☐ no opinion

15. In the last twelve months, did you happen to invite anyone to attend this church?
- ☐ yes
- ☐ no

16. How do you rate the youth program in the following areas:

	excellent	good	only fiar	poor	no opinion
A. helping young people deal with significant issues in their daily lives	☐	☐	☐	☐	☐
B. helping young people to find Christ	☐	☐	☐	☐	☐
C. fun and enjoyment	☐	☐	☐	☐	☐
D. developing significant friendships	☐	☐	☐	☐	☐

Comments:

_____

_____

17. What type of music programs would you emphasize in the allocation of this church's resources?
    - ☐ adult choir/sanctuary choir
    - ☐ youth choir
    - ☐ children's choir
    - ☐ concert recitals
    - ☐ organ/instruments
    - ☐ music in Sunday school
    - ☐ special musical/holiday programs
    - ☐ congregational hymn singing

18. Which of these outreach programs would you like to see this church continue? Check all that apply and then circle the **two** that you consider most important.
    - ☐ crisis ministry
    - ☐ soup kitchen
    - ☐ prison ministry
    - ☐ Meals on Wheels
    - ☐ after-school tutoring and mentoring
    - ☐ counseling ministry

19. Please rate how each of the following aspects of this church's worship services meets your spiritual needs.

	very well	fairly well	not at all well
A. sermon	☐	☐	☐
B. congregational singing	☐	☐	☐
C. choral/special music	☐	☐	☐
D. prayer	☐	☐	☐
E. the Lord's Supper	☐	☐	☐
F. times of silent meditation/reflection	☐	☐	☐
G. testimony	☐	☐	☐
H. worship in community with others	☐	☐	☐

20. How important is it to you personally that the following be included in a sermon?

	very important	fairly important	not at all important
A. relevance to everyday life	☐	☐	☐
B. provoking or stimulating thought	☐	☐	☐
C. biblical content	☐	☐	☐
D. encouraging spiritual growth/direction	☐	☐	☐
E. encouraging witnessing/faith sharing	☐	☐	☐
F. addressing social problems	☐	☐	☐
G. addressing political issues	☐	☐	☐
H. humorous stories/anecdotes	☐	☐	☐

21. How well do you feel these items are dealt with in sermons at this church?

	very well	fairly well	not at all well
A. relevance to everyday life	☐	☐	☐
B. provoking or stimulating thought	☐	☐	☐
C. biblical content	☐	☐	☐
D. encouraging spiritual growth/direction	☐	☐	☐
E. encouraging witnessing/faith sharing	☐	☐	☐
F. addressing social problems	☐	☐	☐
G. addressing political issues	☐	☐	☐
H. humorous stories/anecdotes	☐	☐	☐

22. Here are some words that might be used to describe a church. Please check any of the following words that you feel describes this church.

☐ nurturing	☐ complacent	☐ accepting
☐ energetic	☐ spiritual	☐ friendly
☐ inclusive	☐ intolerant	☐ supportive
☐ sense of direction	☐ easy to get involved	☐ joyful
☐ boring	☐ irrelevant	☐ intimidating
☐ empowering	☐ unfriendly	☐ spontaneous
☐ traditional	☐ innovative	☐ charismatic

☐ other: _____

23. To what extent does worship at this church foster a sense of...

	very well	fairly well	not at all well
A. the presence of God	☐	☐	☐
B. expectancy	☐	☐	☐
C. the awe and mystery of God	☐	☐	☐
D. praise of God	☐	☐	☐
E. petition to God	☐	☐	☐
F. the body of Christ gathered	☐	☐	☐
G. God's forgiveness	☐	☐	☐
H. the love and grace of God	☐	☐	☐
I. healing power of Christ	☐	☐	☐
J. joy	☐	☐	☐

24. Overall, how well do you feel this church sustains and strengthens your faith?
   - ☐ a great deal
   - ☐ quite a lot
   - ☐ somewhat
   - ☐ hardly at all
   - ☐ not at all

25. Which of these statements comes closest to describing your beliefs about Jesus? (Check one)
   - ☐ Jesus was divine in the sense that he was in fact God living among people.
   - ☐ Jesus was divine in the sense that while he was only a person, he was uniquely called by God to reveal God's purpose in the world.
   - ☐ Jesus was divine in that he embodied the best that is in all people.
   - ☐ Jesus was a great man and teacher, but I would not call him divine.
   - ☐ other: _____

26. People give various answers to the question, "What makes a Christian?" Please check those factors that best describe you as a Christian.
- ☐ I was born into a Christian family.
- ☐ I was baptized.
- ☐ I live in a predominately Christian country.
- ☐ I am born again.
- ☐ I have a personal relationship with Jesus Christ.
- ☐ I am affiliated with a Christian church.
- ☐ I attempt to follow Jesus Christ's teachings.
- ☐ I have made a decision to accept Jesus Christ as my Savior and Lord.
- ☐ other: (please specify) _____

27. How important would you say religion is in your own life?
- ☐ very important
- ☐ fairly important
- ☐ not very important
- ☐ don't know

28. Which of these statements comes closest to describing your feelings about the Bible?
- ☐ The Bible is the actual Word of God and is to be taken literally, word for word.
- ☐ The Bible is the inspired Word of God. It contains no errors, but some verses are to be taken symbolically, rather than literally.
- ☐ The Bible is the inspired Word of God, but it may contain historical and scientific errors.
- ☐ The Bible was not inspired by God, but it represents humankind's best understanding of God's nature.
- ☐ The Bible is an ancient book of human fables, legends, history, and moral precepts.

29. In which of these ways would you particularly like to grow? (Check all that apply.)
- ☐ deeper prayer life
- ☐ closer relationship with Jesus Christ
- ☐ more faithful reader of the Bible
- ☐ deeper sense of community with fellow Christians
- ☐ empowerment for social outreach
- ☐ learning how to share my faith with others
- ☐ knowledge of history and traditions of my denomination
- ☐ in discipling others
- ☐ understanding basic Christian beliefs/theology

30. Rate your interest in giving to support these areas of this church's ministry:

	a great deal	some	hardly any	none
A. outreach programs	☐	☐	☐	☐
B. buildings and grounds	☐	☐	☐	☐
C. worship	☐	☐	☐	☐
D. Christian education	☐	☐	☐	☐
E. staff support	☐	☐	☐	☐
F. age-specific ministries (children, youth)	☐	☐	☐	☐
G. endowment	☐	☐	☐	☐

31. Regarding our annual stewardship program, how effective have the following elements been for you:

	very effective	fairly effective	not at all effective
A. biblical teaching	☐	☐	☐
B. budgetary explanation	☐	☐	☐
C. the challenge to give more	☐	☐	☐
D. hearing others' stories of stewardship	☐	☐	☐
E. lessons about tithing	☐	☐	☐
F. viewing financial giving as a faith issue	☐	☐	☐

32. I make a financial contribution to the annual stewardship campaign by:
    - ☐ pledging
    - ☐ contribution to the offering plate
    - ☐ both
    - ☐ neither

33. If none of these, what would you say are the main reasons you choose not to give?

34. Which of these factors are important in your decision on whether or not to volunteer time at this church? (Check all that apply.)
    - ☐ the opportunity to socialize
    - ☐ whether or not the task is short-term
    - ☐ frequency of meetings and planning sessions
    - ☐ whether or not the volunteer work is "hands on"
    - ☐ time of day—daytime, afternoon, or evening
    - ☐ child-care situation
    - ☐ the spiritual growth that can come in helping others
    - ☐ the extent to which individuals or groups are recognized and appreciated

35. Which **five** of the following do you consider to be the most important goals for this church? (Check only five.)
- ☐ encourage a stronger commitment to Jesus Christ
- ☐ deepen prayer life among church members
- ☐ increase biblical understanding
- ☐ increase social outreach to the community
- ☐ strengthen the sense of community within the church family
- ☐ deepen the understanding of stewardship
- ☐ raise the level of financial giving
- ☐ increase the knowledge of the traditions of this denomination
- ☐ improve church facilities
- ☐ expand music ministries
- ☐ increase membership
- ☐ expand adult education
- ☐ expand lay ministries
- ☐ increase awareness of social concerns
- ☐ strengthen small group/neighborhood programs
- ☐ expand the diversity of this church's membership
- ☐ provide opportunities for helping others to mature in faith

36. What do you believe is God's vision for this church?

37. Which **one** of the following do you think should be this church's top priority?
- ☐ proclaiming the Gospel
- ☐ adding members
- ☐ spiritual care of church members
- ☐ service to the community
- ☐ changing society

Background Information
1. Gender:
- ☐ male
- ☐ female

2. Age: _____

3. Family status: (Check any that apply.)
- ☐ single
- ☐ married
- ☐ divorced
- ☐ separated
- ☐ widowed
- ☐ children at home
- ☐ parents/elderly at home
- ☐ disabled at home

4. Please check any of the following that apply to those who live in your household:
- ☐ child[ren] 6 years or less
- ☐ child[ren] 7-12 years
- ☐ child[ren] 13-17 years
- ☐ young adults (18 years and older) living at home
- ☐ young adults (18 years and older) away at school
- ☐ parents 65 years and older

5. Your education: (Check last level completed.)
- ☐ grades 1-11
- ☐ high school graduate
- ☐ technical/trade school
- ☐ some college
- ☐ college graduate
- ☐ some postgraduate work
- ☐ master's/professional degree
- ☐ doctoral degree

6. Current employment status: (Check only one.)
- ☐ full time
- ☐ part time
- ☐ student
- ☐ homemaker
- ☐ unemployed
- ☐ retired
- ☐ other (please specify): _____

7. How long have you lived in this area?
- ☐ under 1 year
- ☐ 1-5 years
- ☐ 6-10 years
- ☐ 11-15 years
- ☐ more than 15 years

8. How many years have you been coming to this church? _____

9. How frequently do you attend services? (Check one.)
- ☐ at least once a week
- ☐ several times a month
- ☐ about once a month
- ☐ less than once a month

10. Which Sunday service do you attend **most often?** (Check one.)
- ☐ 8:00 a.m.
- ☐ 9:00 a.m.
- ☐ 11:15 a.m.
- ☐ no particular service

11. In which denomination were you primarily raised? (Check one.)
    □ Baptist
    □ Episcopalian
    □ Lutheran
    □ Presbyterian
    □ Roman Catholic
    □ United Church of Christ/Congregational
    □ United Methodist
    □ other (please specify): _____

12. How long have you been involved in this denomination? (Check one that is closest approximation.)
    □ 2 years
    □ 5 years
    □ 10 years
    □ 20 years
    □ 30 years
    □ 40 years
    □ 50 years

13. If you have children in Sunday school, please indicate below how many in each category listed. (If none, please skip this question.)
    __ nursery   __ preschool   __ grades K-5
    __ grades 6-9   __ grades 10-12   __ college

14. How actively involved are you in your church and in church activities?
    □ a great deal
    □ somewhat
    □ hardly at all
    □ not at all

15. Do you consider yourself more active or less active at this church now than you were five years ago?
    □ more
    □ less
    □ same

16. How effective are this church's publications in communicating information to you?

	excellent	good	fair	poor
A. church newsletter	□	□	□	□
B. worship bulletin	□	□	□	□

In closing, please include any additional thoughts you have about this church:

Permission to photocopy this survey granted for local church use. Copyright © George H. Gallup Jr. and D. Michael Lindsay. Published in *The Gallup Guide: Reality Check for 21st Century Churches* by Group Publishing, Inc., P.O. Box 481, Loveland, CO 80539. www.grouppublishing.com

Survey 9

1. During the past two years, have you done any of the following? (Read)

   Yes No

   A. ☐ ☐ volunteered time to help poor or needy people
   B. ☐ ☐ regularly read a newspaper
   C. ☐ ☐ discussed political issues or social problems with friends
   D. ☐ ☐ participated in a class or study group, in a church or synagogue
   E. ☐ ☐ studied, either individually or with others, one or more major social problems, such as peace, racism, or sexism
   F. ☐ ☐ read a book dealing with finding more meaning in life
   G. ☐ ☐ attended religious services at least once a month
   H. ☐ ☐ served on a church or synagogue board or committee
   I. ☐ ☐ been involved in political or community social action projects

2. I am going to read you two statements. Please tell me which one best describes your own opinion.

   A. ☐ A person's faith *should not* change throughout life, because it is the foundation for living.

   or

   B. ☐ A person's faith *should* change throughout life, just as one's body and mind change.

For each "yes" response to Question 3, Questions 4 and 5 are to be asked.

3. During your lifetime, have you ever:

4. Please tell me whether the experience affected your thoughts about the meaning and purpose of life a great deal, some, or not at all. (If respondent had experience more than once, ask about the most memorable or significant experience.)

5. How old were you when this happened? (Best estimate acceptable)

	Question 3		Question 4				Question 5
A. received a promotion or honor at work?	yes	no	a great deal	some	not at all	don't know/ no answer	age ____
B. had a baby (as father *or* mother)?	yes	no	a great deal	some	not at all	don't know/ no answer	age ____
C. had a divorce?	yes	no	a great deal	some	not at all	don't know/ no answer	age ____
D. experienced the death of a loved one?	yes	no	a great deal	some	not at all	don't know/ no answer	age ____
E. been lonely for a long period of time?	yes	no	a great deal	some	not at all	don't know/ no answer	age ____

	Question 3	Question 4	Question 5
F. had a "born again" experience?	yes no	a great deal some not at all don't know/ no answer	age ____
G. been seriously worried about your health?	yes no	a great deal some not at all don't know/ no answer	age ____
H. been out of work for a long period of time?	yes no	a great deal some not at all don't know/ no answer	age ____
I. considered an abortion for yourself or someone close to you?	yes no	a great deal some not at all don't know/ no answer	age ____
J. made the conscious decision to leave a church or religious group?	yes no	a great deal some not at all don't know/ no answer	age ____
K. received counseling for emotional difficulty?	yes no	a great deal some not at all don't know/ no answer	age ____

Ask everyone:

6. When you are faced with a problem or crisis, like those in the previous question, to which of the following kinds of support would you likely turn for help?

Yes No
A. ☐ ☐ share it with family
B. ☐ ☐ share it with close friends
C. ☐ ☐ discuss it with a class or a group in your church or synagogue
D. ☐ ☐ work through it on your own
E. ☐ ☐ read the Bible or other inspired literature
F. ☐ ☐ seek help from a religious counselor
G. ☐ ☐ seek other professional counseling
H. ☐ ☐ seek help from a support group
I. ☐ ☐ pray about it

7. How much have you *thought* about each of the following during the past two years: a lot, a fair amount, only a little, or not at all?

	a lot	a fair amount	only a little	not at all	don't know/ no answer
A. your relationship to God	☐	☐	☐	☐	☐
B. living a worthwhile life	☐	☐	☐	☐	☐
C. developing your faith	☐	☐	☐	☐	☐
D. the basic meaning and value of your life	☐	☐	☐	☐	☐

8. Which *one* of the following four statements comes closest to your own view of "faith"? (Read all statements before response is accepted; must choose only one—if necessary, ask respondent, "Which *one* of these comes closest to your own view?"

    A. ☐ a set of beliefs
    B. ☐ membership in a church or synagogue
    C. ☐ finding meaning in life
    D. ☐ a relationship with God

9. Imagine a five-point scale where "1" is a person you would describe as having little or no faith and "5" is a person with a great deal of faith. Where would you place yourself on this scale? You may choose any number from one to five.

    Little or no faith 1   2   3   4   5   A great deal of faith

10. Using the same five-point scale, where would you place yourself at about the age of sixteen?

    Little or no faith 1   2   3   4   5   A great deal of faith

11. How important is religion in your own life—would you say not important, fairly unimportant, fairly important, or very important?

    ☐ not important
    ☐ fairly unimportant
    ☐ fairly important
    ☐ very important

12. How important to you is the belief that your life has meaning or has a purpose?

    ☐ not important
    ☐ fairly unimportant
    ☐ fairly important
    ☐ very important

13. Would you say your experience with religion during your lifetime has been…

    ☐ very positive
    ☐ somewhat positive
    ☐ neither negative nor positive
    ☐ somewhat negative
    ☐ very negative

14. I am going to read you some statements. For each I would like you to tell me how much you agree or disagree with the statement using a five-point scale. If "5" on the scale means you strongly agree and "1" means you strongly disagree, where would you place yourself? Remember you may use any whole number from one to five.

	strongly disagree				strongly agree
A. I feel close to God when I participate in a service of worship.	1	2	3	4	5
B. I sometimes wonder about the existence of God.	1	2	3	4	5
C. God punishes bad people.	1	2	3	4	5

	strongly disagree				strongly agree
D. The human mind can never fully understand God.	1	2	3	4	5
E. God is the name we have given to the intelligence of the universe.	1	2	3	4	5
F. You have to go to church to practice religious ritual if you expect God to do anything for you.	1	2	3	4	5
G. People should just believe in God and not argue about religion.	1	2	3	4	5
H. God reveals himself through a variety of religious beliefs and traditions.	1	2	3	4	5

15. Now, which of these two statements best describes your own opinion?
    ☐ A person's faith is usually strengthened by questioning early beliefs.
    or
    ☐ A person's faith is usually weakened by questioning early beliefs.

16. In terms of your own definition of "faith," would you say your faith changed significantly... (Multiple answers accepted.)
    ☐ in the past 5 years
    ☐ in the past 6-10 years
    ☐ in the past 10-20 years
    ☐ more than 20 years ago
    ☐ never (Go to question 21.)

17. About how old were you when your faith changed significantly? (Best estimate. If more than one answer above, accept multiple answers here.)
    _____ _____ _____

18. Which of these words or phrases best describes your faith as a result of the change? Is it... (Record response for each pair of phrases.)
    ☐ stronger   or   ☐ weaker
    ☐ less meaningful   or   ☐ more meaningful
    ☐ totally different   or   ☐ a little different

19. Would you describe the change mostly as...
    ☐ coming about as a result of a lot of thought and discussion about faith
    or
    ☐ coming about as a result of a strong emotional experience

20. Would you say the change...(Choose one.)
    ☐ came at a time when your life was essentially "stable" or "normal"
    or
    ☐ came at a time when your life was "turbulent" or "chaotic"

21. What is your religious preference?
- ☐ Roman Catholic (Go to question 23.)
- ☐ Mainline Protestant
- ☐ Jewish
- ☐ Orthodox
- ☐ Evangelical
- ☐ Humanist
- ☐ Mormon (Go to question 23.)
- ☐ other (please specify): _____
- ☐ none (Go to question 25.)

22. Within your general religious preference, do you have a specific affiliation (denomination)? If so, what is it?

23. Are you a member of or actively related to a church, synagogue, or other organization of your religious preference?
- ☐ yes
- ☐ no

24. Do you consider yourself more active or less active now than you were ten years ago?
- ☐ more
- ☐ less

25. What sort of things, if any, do you do to nourish or strengthen your faith or sense of meaning in life?
- ☐ pray or meditate alone
- ☐ attend religious services
- ☐ study the Bible or religious topics in a church class or study group
- ☐ discuss personal problems with a pastor or other religious counselor
- ☐ watch religious TV
- ☐ read the Bible or other religious books
- ☐ participate in a prayer group
- ☐ deal with personal problems on your own

Permission to photocopy this survey granted for local church use. Copyright © George H. Gallup Jr. and D. Michael Lindsay. Published in *The Gallup Guide: Reality Check for 21st Century Churches* by Group Publishing, Inc., P.O. Box 481, Loveland, CO 80539. www.grouppublishing.com

Survey 10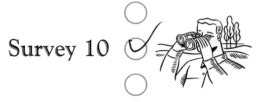

Views About the New Pastor

1. Please describe—fully and frankly—the kind of person (in terms of traits, skills, and background) you think would be the ideal new leader of this church.

2. How important—very, fairly, not at all—is it that the new pastor have the following traits, skills, or background characteristics?

	very	fairly	not at all	no opinion
A. have effective pastoral skills	☐	☐	☐	☐
B. be a knowledgeable and effective preacher	☐	☐	☐	☐
C. be open in sharing his or her faith	☐	☐	☐	☐
D. be able to relate to all ages in teaching and counseling	☐	☐	☐	☐
E. will make the Bible relevant to daily lives of parishioners	☐	☐	☐	☐
F. will encourage programs to bring new members to the church	☐	☐	☐	☐
G. will emphasize community outreach	☐	☐	☐	☐
H. have good administrative skills	☐	☐	☐	☐
I. have a deep, personal relationship with Jesus Christ	☐	☐	☐	☐
J. work toward the further conversion of unbelievers	☐	☐	☐	☐
K. has a good working relationship with the lay leadership	☐	☐	☐	☐
L. emphasizes small groups that meet for prayer and Bible study	☐	☐	☐	☐
M. teach adult forums and classes	☐	☐	☐	☐
N. visit church members regularly	☐	☐	☐	☐
O. encourages people to develop a deep, personal relationship with Jesus Christ	☐	☐	☐	☐
P. be open to new expressions of worship	☐	☐	☐	☐
Q. participate in a small group	☐	☐	☐	☐
R. help church members develop their prayer lives	☐	☐	☐	☐
S. is interested in developing better stewardship	☐	☐	☐	☐

T. takes an active role in groups that address social issues	☐	☐	☐	☐
U. works closely with other churches in the community	☐	☐	☐	☐
V. encourage programs for the poor and hungry	☐	☐	☐	☐
W. is interested in encouraging personal spiritual growth at this church	☐	☐	☐	☐
X. encourages evangelism	☐	☐	☐	☐
Y. encourages lay leadership	☐	☐	☐	☐

3. What age should the new pastor be; does it make any difference to you?
   - ☐ under 40 years
   - ☐ 40 to 50 years
   - ☐ over 50 years
   - ☐ makes no difference

4. And what gender?
   - ☐ female
   - ☐ male
   - ☐ makes no difference

5. In which of the following fields, if any, should the new pastor have special training or experience?
   - ☐ ministry to alcoholics
   - ☐ ministry to drug addicts
   - ☐ ministry to the handicapped
   - ☐ Christian education
   - ☐ ministry to single persons
   - ☐ music
   - ☐ arts/drama
   - ☐ ministry to youth
   - ☐ ministry to aged
   - ☐ counseling/psychology
   - ☐ crisis intervention
   - ☐ ministry to divorced persons
   - ☐ hunger ministry
   - ☐ urban ministry
   - ☐ business administration, computers
   - ☐ fund raising
   - ☐ ministry to minorities

Views About This Church

6. What do you regard as the greatest strengths of this church—that is, what makes it special?

7. And what do you regard as areas that need improvement at this church?

8. What are we like as a church community?

9. What would you like this church to be in the years ahead?

10. Which **five** of the following do you consider to be the most important goals for this church?

☐ encourage a stronger commitment to Jesus Christ on the part of the parishioners

☐ deepen prayer life among parishioners

☐ increase biblical knowledge

☐ deepen the understanding of stewardship

☐ better equip people for evangelism

☐ increase social outreach to the community

☐ bring about more unity among the people

☐ support a mission or a missionary

☐ raise the level of financial giving

☐ increase knowledge of the traditions of the church

☐ increase awareness of social issues

☐ grow in number of church members

☐ improve facilities

☐ encourage development of small groups

☐ expand Bible study

☐ further develop youth programs

☐ place greater emphasis on lay ministry

☐ stress adult education

☐ encourage people to speak more freely about their faith journeys

☐ create stronger bonds with other churches of our denomination in the area

☐ encourage a program of invitation to new people

☐ encourage a greater lay ministry among church members

☐ develop a strong neighborhood program

☐ increase number of minorities among this church's membership

11. Do the Sunday services meet your worship needs?

☐ yes, completely

☐ yes, mostly

☐ no

12. In what ways could they better meet your worship needs? (Please comment on all aspects, including music and prayer.)

Religious Beliefs/Practices

13. How would you describe your own belief in/relationship to Jesus Christ?

14. Which one of these statements comes closest to describing your beliefs about Jesus?
    - ☐ Jesus was divine in the sense that he was in fact God living among people.
    - ☐ Jesus was divine in the sense that while he was only a person, he was uniquely called by God to reveal God's purpose in the world.
    - ☐ Jesus was divine in that he embodied the best that is in all people.
    - ☐ Jesus was a great man and teacher, but I would not call him divine.
    - ☐ other: _____

15. To what extent do you believe that Jesus Christ is the incarnate Son of God and that he has done everything necessary for your salvation?
    - ☐ believe completely
    - ☐ believe for the most part
    - ☐ do not believe
    - ☐ no opinion

16. How important is each of the following as a reason for your attending this church?

	very	fairly	not at all	no opinion
A. sermons	☐	☐	☐	☐
B. fellowship/friendship	☐	☐	☐	☐
C. spiritual guidance and renewal	☐	☐	☐	☐
D. religious education—adults	☐	☐	☐	☐
E. religious education—youth	☐	☐	☐	☐
F. music and choir	☐	☐	☐	☐
G. the liturgy	☐	☐	☐	☐
H. to be part of a worshipping community	☐	☐	☐	☐
I. the sacraments	☐	☐	☐	☐
J. other:_____				

17. Approximately how many times did you attend worship services at this church in the last twelve months?
    - ☐ none
    - ☐ 1-10
    - ☐ 11-25
    - ☐ 26-39
    - ☐ 40 and over

18. Do you set aside time for prayer on a regular basis?
    ☐ yes
    ☐ no

19. Do you read the Bible on a regular basis?
    ☐ yes
    ☐ no

20. (If yes to question 19) Do you read it as part of your regular devotions?
    ☐ yes
    ☐ no

21. How important would you say your Christian faith is in your life?
    ☐ very important
    ☐ fairly important
    ☐ not very important
    ☐ not at all important
    ☐ don't know

22. Have you participated in any Bible study or prayer group, or do you intend to?
    ☐ yes, have participated
       Which? _____
    ☐ no, but intend to
       Which? _____
    ☐ no, not interested

23. Do think that financial support of the church by tithing is a goal toward which the church should work?
    ☐ yes
    ☐ no
    ☐ no opinion

24. You will notice that the numbers go from "1," for something you *strongly disagree* with, to "5," for something you *strongly agree* with. Using this scale, please tell me how strongly you agree or disagree with each of the following statements.

	strongly disagree				**strongly agree**
A. I wish my relationship with other Christians was stronger.	1	2	3	4	5
B. I try to bring others to Christ through the way I live or through discussion or prayer.	1	2	3	4	5
C. God gives me the strength that I would not otherwise have to forgive people who have hurt me deeply.	1	2	3	4	5

	strongly disagree			strongly agree	
D. I do things I don't want to do because I believe it is the will of God.	1	2	3	4	5
E. I believe in the full authority of the Bible.	1	2	3	4	5
F. I wish my religious beliefs were stronger.	1	2	3	4	5
G. I believe that Jesus Christ was fully human and fully divine.	1	2	3	4	5
H. I receive comfort and support from my religious beliefs.	1	2	3	4	5
I. I try hard to put my religious beliefs into practice in my relations with all people, regardless of their backgrounds.	1	2	3	4	5
J. I believe that God loves me even though I may not always obey him.	1	2	3	4	5
K. I seek God's will through prayer.	1	2	3	4	5
L. My religious faith is the most important influence in my life.	1	2	3	4	5

Permission to photocopy this survey granted for local church use. Copyright © George H. Gallup Jr. and D. Michael Lindsay. Published in *The Gallup Guide: Reality Check for 21st Century Churches* by Group Publishing, Inc., P.O. Box 481, Loveland, CO 80539. www.grouppublishing.com

Bonus Demographic Questionnaire

General Demographic Questions for Any Survey

1. What is your gender?
   - ☐ male
   - ☐ female

2. What is your age?
   - ☐ 18-29 years
   - ☐ 30-49 years
   - ☐ 50-64 years
   - ☐ 65 years and over

3. What is the highest level of education have you completed?
   - ☐ some high school
   - ☐ high school graduate
   - ☐ some college
   - ☐ trade/technical/vocational training
   - ☐ college graduate
   - ☐ some postgraduate study
   - ☐ postgraduate degree
   - ☐ don't know

4. What is your religious preference?
   - ☐ Protestant
   - ☐ Roman Catholic
   - ☐ Jewish
   - ☐ an Orthodox church such as the Greek or Russian Orthodox Church
   - ☐ Seventh-Day Adventist
   - ☐ Christian Scientist
   - ☐ Mormon
   - ☐ Muslim
   - ☐ something else (please specify)
   - ☐ don't know/refused

5. If Protestant, ask: Which denomination is that?

6. Would you describe yourself as a "born-again" or evangelical Christian?
   - ☐ yes
   - ☐ no
   - ☐ don't know/refused

7. Do you happen to be a member of a church, synagogue, mosque, or other organized religious group?
  - ☐ yes
  - ☐ no
  - ☐ don't know/refused

8. Did you happen to attend church, synagogue, mosque, or some other religious worship service in the last seven days?
  - ☐ yes, did attend
  - ☐ no, did not attend
  - ☐ don't know/refused

9. Ethnicity: We want to be sure that we have spoken to a broad mix of people in your area. Are you, yourself, of Hispanic origin or descent, such as Mexican, Puerto Rican, Cuban, or other Spanish background?
  - ☐ yes
  - ☐ no
  - ☐ don't know/refused

10. Race: What is your race? Are you white, African-American, or some other race?
  - ☐ white
  - ☐ African-American
  - ☐ other (please specify)
  - ☐ don't know/refused

   Note: The U.S. Census Bureau distinguishes ethnicity and race. Often, while conducting Gallup surveys, respondents of Hispanic origin will classify their race as "Hispanic." However, according to the Census Bureau, Hispanic is a category for ethnicity, not race. As a result, we usually ask a question to determine if the respondent is of Hispanic origin. Then, we ask a follow-up question about race. This increases the response rate for the race question. In other words, respondents of Hispanic origin are likelier to answer the question on race using the Census Bureau's categories after first being asked about their ethnicity.

11. Is your total annual income before taxes $20,000 or more, or is it less than $20,000?
   (If under, ask:) Is it over or under $15,000?
   (If under, ask:) Is it over or under $10,000?
   (If over, ask:) Is it over or under $30,000?
   (If over, ask:) Is it over or under $50,000?
   (If over, ask:) Is it over or under $75,000?

   (Mark response category below.)
  - ☐ Less than $10,000
  - ☐ $10,000-$14,999
  - ☐ $15,000-$19,999
  - ☐ $20,000-$29,999
  - ☐ $30,000-$49,999
  - ☐ $50,000-$74,999
  - ☐ $75,000 and over
  - ☐ don't know/refused

12. Are you now employed full-time, part-time, not employed, or retired?
- ☐ full-time
- ☐ part-time
- ☐ not employed
- ☐ retired
- ☐ no answer/refused

13. Including yourself, how many people live within your household?

14. Are there any children under the age of eighteen years currently living in your household?
- ☐ yes
- ☐ no
- ☐ don't know/refused

15. What is your marital status?
- ☐ single/never been married
- ☐ married
- ☐ separated
- ☐ divorced
- ☐ widowed
- ☐ don't know/refused

16. How would you describe your political views?
- ☐ very conservative
- ☐ conservative
- ☐ moderate
- ☐ liberal
- ☐ very liberal
- ☐ don't know/refused

Permission to photocopy this survey granted for local church use. Copyright © George H. Gallup Jr. and D. Michael Lindsay. Published in *The Gallup Guide: Reality Check for 21st Century Churches* by Group Publishing, Inc., P.O. Box 481, Loveland, CO 80539. www.grouppublishing.com

Chapter Five

Reducing Error in the Study

E very research study seeks validity and reliability. Reliability refers to the likelihood of arriving at the same results if the survey were repeated. It sug- gests that a survey administered in January will reach the same conclusions if administered to a similar group in July. Validity entails that the question accurately measures an item of interest and that the respondent interprets the question as the survey team intended. In other words, a valid survey is precise, and a reliable sur- vey is consistent. Survey error occurs when valid, reliable data is not achieved, either through fault or neglect. In this regard, survey error includes mistakes such as incorrectly recording answers during an interview, but it is also broader than this. One important component of survey error is bias. Bias occurs when a meas- urement is consistently higher or lower than the measurement's true value. For example, answers will vary if we ask people, "How long have you been a member of this church?" Some individuals will immediately remember when they joined the church and will be able to provide the true number of years they have been members. Others will estimate, indiscriminately rounding up or down according to their best recollection. Some will think they know exactly, but they will be mis- taken, perhaps remembering when they moved to the community but forgetting that they did not join the church until one year later. All of these errors, none of which are intentional or malicious, introduce bias into the survey. The challenge facing the survey team is to minimize the survey's bias as much as possible. Typically, this involves addressing two main sources of errors: data collection and interviewers.

DATA COLLECTION ERRORS

Regardless of the form of data collection (mail, telephone, or personal inter- view), there are a number of possible sources of error. One key source is, of course, non-response on the part of the prospective respondent. This is called "unit non-response." There are various ways to minimize the degree of this error. This usually requires professional assistance and can be a costly endeavor for the church, so sample surveys are beyond the scope of this book. We recommend a survey of the entire population (earlier mentioned as the survey universe) that is similar to a census. Every person in the population is asked to participate in the survey, or every person in a particular group. Perhaps the survey team would like to ask the women of the

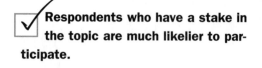 **Respondents who have a stake in the topic are much likelier to participate.**

church their opinions on the women's and children's ministries. Or maybe you want to solicit the opinions of parents of teenagers in the church.

What, then, can we do to solicit a greater measure of respondent participation? First, questionnaires must be presented as interesting and important to the respondent. Respondents who have a stake in the topic are much likelier to participate. Second, the survey team ought to employ effective data collection procedures such as advance and cover letters. Third, pay close attention to the rate of non-response when conducting the pretest. Typically, non-response is not random; there may be certain types of people who are less likely to participate in the survey, for whatever reasons. For example, young professional women may not be as interested in another church obligation, which they may perceive as inherent in a women's ministry. As a result, this subgroup of the population (women members) may choose not to complete the survey after learning in the introduction that the survey is designed to help the church begin a new women's ministry. Identifying in the pretest the characteristics of those who are less likely to cooperate is extremely helpful in reducing unit non-response for the survey. If the team notices a trend, we suggest a follow-up conversation with a few participants who refused to participate in hopes of rectifying what caused them not to participate. Perhaps it was a matter of bad timing, but if consistent trends appear along demographic lines, there is probably more going on.

Simply stated, the survey project must be perceived by the respondent as relevant. Because the participant is donating his time by completing the survey, he or she needs to be convinced that the survey is worthwhile. The survey team must work strategically to persuade participants that the questionnaire's topic is relevant to their lives and that the questions being asked address the topic adequately. One good rule of thumb is if you cannot decide how the data will be used, do not ask the question. Designing a questionnaire that is succinct, complete, and important for the respondent will greatly help increase the rate of response. Perhaps most important is a liberal use of phrases such as "we gratefully appreciate your participation," "thank you in advance for your participation," and "your participation makes such a difference; thank you" in all forms of communication with the respondents.

The single most effective method of reducing unit non-response is the callback method. This involves attempting additional contact with participants who are not reached on the first attempt. When conducting a mail survey, research has shown that varying the method of contact increases the unit response rate.

This was referred to earlier as mixed mode methodology. For example, if you know the participants from whom you have not yet received their questionnaires from a mail survey, you

☒ **The single most effective method of reducing unit non-response is the callback method.**

might enlist several interviewers to call those individuals and conduct the follow-up survey over the telephone. If your church wants to continue with additional mail correspondence, you might send a follow-up postcard a few weeks after the original survey and cover letter were sent.

For those who remain unresponsive, a second, different cover letter might be sent a few weeks later. We include some sample letters in the next chapter. Remember to include another copy of the survey in case the respondent has misplaced or lost his or her copy. This method of repeated contact only works if the survey team is recording the return of each questionnaire. It only makes economic sense to wait until the responses dwindle before attempting a subsequent contact.

Some people will respond immediately to a mail questionnaire. This is followed by a period of several days in which there is a relatively high number of returns with approximately the same number of returns each day. At some point the survey team will notice that questionnaire returns have trickled off; at which time we recommend an additional contact. Continue this practice until the survey team is satisfied with the rate of response.

Monetary or gift incentives can be effective ways to enlist participation. Market researchers will sometimes include a one-dollar bill with each mailed questionnaire to elicit a higher response rate. Although a bit unconventional for church surveys, this method might be amended to increase the rate of response. The church could consider offering one-dollar vouchers for use at the church bookstore or at a fellowship meal; also it is important to stress that the voucher or money is a mere token of appreciation. Otherwise, respondents might resent the suggestion that their time is worth so little. The token of appreciation conveys a sense of trust that the surveyor has in the respondent—trust that he or she will accept an offer made in good faith in exchange for his or her participation.

Unit non-response involves several unique challenges when conducting a telephone survey. Most participants decide to participate or not within the first minute of a telephone survey, and often their participation is more the absence of a decision not to participate than the willful decision to participate. Whenever the interviewer records a unit non-response, he or she must record careful notes regarding the circumstances of the non-response. Was the intended participant simply not home? Did the interviewer only reach an answering machine? Did the individual explicitly refuse to participate? Recording these circumstances as well as the time, date, and day of the week contact was sought will be instrumental for the survey team's subsequent follow-up attempts to enlist cooperation with the survey. Studies show that the average number of contact attempts for telephone surveys range from three to twenty; we recommend at least five attempts for a church survey. In addition to the key role of interviewer training (discussed below), there are several techniques that have proven effective in achieving a higher response rate. These include the following:

- ◆ scheduling appointments for callbacks;
- ◆ attempting callbacks at different times of the day and different days of the week than earlier, unsuccessful attempts;
- ◆ mailing the questionnaire to the respondent if he or she is never reached by phone; and
- ◆ identifying if lack of English knowledge is contributing to non-response, and offering to conduct the survey in the respondent's native language.

Item non-response refers to unanswered questions, and these also tend to occur in certain patterns. Frequently, respondents are reluctant to answer certain questions, especially on items relating to demographic profile (age, income, level of education). The interviewer can play an important role in allaying the respondent's concerns. Saying something like "We are gathering this information for analysis purposes; your responses will not be linked to your name, telephone number, or your address." Also, interviewers should remind reluctant respondents that their responses are kept strictly confidential. Since this type of interaction is not possible with mail surveys, the pretest becomes even more critical to minimizing item non-response with this method of data collection. Special attention should be paid if certain items are consistently unmarked on the pretest questionnaire; perhaps the item is laid out on

> ✓ **Special attention should be paid if certain items are consistently unmarked on the pretest questionnaire.**

WHAT MAKES A GOOD INTERVIEWER?

 Traditionally, demographic characteristics such as age, gender, and region of the country do not greatly affect one's ability to conduct effective survey interviews. Instead, good interviewers have the following:

- ◆ **Interpersonal engagement that is responsive and persuasive—** strong interpersonal skills in conversation are extremely important for both in-person and telephone interviews.

- ◆ **Confidence in the survey's importance—**this confidence, in turn, helps convince the respondent that he or she should participate.

- ◆ **A sort of "sixth sense" of liking the challenge of completing a job they think is important to them, but being sensitive to the wishes and time constraints of survey respondents.**

We recommend a day-long training seminar for interviewers that instructs them on general interviewing techniques, as well as the particular topic being explored with the survey. Interviewers are the survey team's representatives to the respondents, so they must be extremely well informed on the purpose of the study, as well as how its results will be used and reported.

the page in an obscure or unnoticeable place, which may contribute to item non-response.

> ☒ **All interviews ought to be conducted with the same script to ensure reliability.**

INTERVIEWERS AND ERROR

We cannot overstate the importance of interviewers closely following the survey script. Deviations of any form—whether making personal remarks or offering explanations that are not part of the survey—will introduce additional error into the study. As a result, the survey team must remain vigilant in insisting that interviewers read the survey script verbatim, including the introduction, questions and categories of response, and transitions between sections. No matter how well-intentioned the interviewer may be in offering additional comments or personal stories, their inclusion biases the survey and increases its margin of error. All interviews ought to be conducted with the same script to ensure reliability. The most difficult part of this task emerges when the interviewer has to deviate from the script because of the respondent's comments. From soliciting cooperation in the beginning to probing for greater clarification during the survey, the interviewer must be adept at handling various situations without unduly introducing more error to the project. In addition, the interviewer must not offer any judgments on responses, for this may skew the validity of the answers. Effective training is the best tool for accomplishing these goals.

Certain individuals appear to be endowed with the interpersonal skills needed to be effective interviewers, while some are not. The pretesting process can be very helpful in determining those individuals who are best suited for interviewing. For a church survey, you will probably rely on the work of volunteers, so it will be even more important that the appropriate individuals are selected to conduct the

---

KEY PARTS OF THE INTERVIEWERS' TRAINING SEMINAR

- ◆ Learning the purpose, scope, and sponsorship of the survey with detailed information about how the data will be used and how confidentiality is maintained

- ◆ Knowing the steps to contacting respondents and eliciting their participation

- ◆ Practicing interview sessions by reading through the survey, paying attention to various "skip" patterns

- ◆ Exploring ways to probe for inadequate answers without passing judgment

- ◆ Learning how to record answers and code open-ended responses

- ◆ Understanding guidelines for handling various interpersonal challenges that may arise during an interview

- ◆ Role-playing particular objections to survey participation or certain aspects of the questionnaire

interviews. Screening all interested volunteers for the job during the pretest is an effective way of determining the best interviewers. For those not as well suited to interviewing, a number of important tasks remain, including data entry and quality control, as well as other assignments.

> ✓ **The cardinal rule in enlisting respondent cooperation is to engage them in the process early in the survey, moving quickly into the first question.**

The seminar should include numerous opportunities for interviewers to role-play the interview, devoting some time to potential problems regarding unit or item non-response. For instance, if you are conducting a survey of the congregation's opinion on worship styles, the interviewers will need precise definitions for terms used in the survey (such as *contemporary* and *traditional worship style*). The interviewers should practice reading the survey script several times, mastering finer points in pronunciation, rate of reading, and pauses. The more familiar the interviewer is with the survey script, the less likely an unusual response will fluster the interviewer. Two simple instructions for the survey script involve response categories. During the training seminar, tell the interviewers not to mention the number code listed beside each response category; this becomes tedious for the respondent and is unnecessary.

Most interviewers want to know how to handle difficult situations that can occur frequently. The goal is to create a team of standardized interviewers, ones that ask questions the same way every time and respond in similar fashion quite consistently to any respondent's questions or reaction to the survey. Instilling a sense of standardization among the interviewing team is a vital component for the day-long seminar, and we suggest discussing and role-playing common challenges that often thwart the goal of a standardized interview. In the table on page 145 we have identified several typical situations involving reluctant respondents with a few recommendations.

The survey team might decide to produce a fact sheet similar to this table that contains the appropriate responses to participants' comments and questions, as well as important details about the survey's sponsorship, purpose, and use of the data gathered. The cardinal rule in enlisting respondent cooperation is to engage them in the process early in the survey, moving quickly into the first question.

Listen for the specific reason the participant offers for not participating, and try to determine what can be done to enlist participation (calling back at another time or scheduling an appointment, for example).

Once the respondent agrees to participate in the survey, one of three problems may occur. These include the respondent not answering with one of the response categories provided, the respondent asking another question instead of answering the survey item, and the respondent making a comment without

RESPONDENT SAYS...	POSSIBLE RESPONSE
"This is a bad time."	"I understand. May I call you later today or another day this week? We very much want your input."
"I don't know anything about that topic."	"We are just looking for people's opinions and thoughts. You don't need to know anything about this topic to complete the survey. There are no right or wrong answers."
"Is this conversation confidential?"	"Absolutely! Names are not associated with particular respondents' answers, so rest assured, your comments cannot be linked to your name. The final report will reveal the responses gathered from all of the interviews, so no individual responses can ever be identified."
"It's no one's business what I think."	"I understand, and that's why we keep all responses confidential. Maintaining your privacy is one of our top priorities. I can assure you that the results will be released in such a way that no single individual can ever be identified. We separate people's names from their responses, and we promise to maintain your privacy."
"I'm sick, and this is a bad time."	"I'm so sorry to hear that. I would be happy to call back in a few days. Would that be better?"
"We don't take sales calls at home."	"I have nothing to sell. As I mentioned, I'm calling from Lassen Road United Methodist Church, and we simply want to hear the opinions of people like you."
"I'm not a religious person."	"That's great. You're just the type of person we need for this survey."
"My husband (wife) is unavailable and isn't interested in the survey."	Call back at a different time of day in hopes of avoiding the telephone gatekeeper.

answering the question. In each of these circumstances, the skilled interviewer will probe for a meaningful response that can be coded according to the response categories. Probing can involve several techniques, including

◆ repeating the question.

◆ repeating the answer (especially if the interviewer is uncertain he or she understood the respondent correctly).

◆ indicating interest and understanding (saying "yes" and "I see," but being careful not to say "good" so as to indicate approval for a particular response).

◆ asking a neutral question such as "How do you mean that?" or "Could you be more specific?" This works especially well for open-ended questions.

The following is a common interviewing situation that necessitates additional probing. Below is a question with the corresponding answers.

In your opinion, how important is the type of music in setting the tone for a worship service?

1. ☐ very important

2. ☐ somewhat important

3. ☐ not very important

4. ☐ not at all important

Suppose the respondent answers with "important." That response does not correspond to any of the answer categories, so the interviewer must probe for greater clarification. A skilled interviewer will recognize that the response excludes categories 3 and 4, so he or she would probe by saying, "By saying it's important, would that be 'very important' or 'somewhat important'?"

Additional problems may arise during the interview process, so dedicate a portion of the training seminar to addressing some of the concerns detailed in the chart on the next page.

INVOLVING THE CONGREGATION

Although many members of the congregation may be aware that a survey is planned and some will help organize it, your survey will be more successful if it is publicized widely. Not only will more people participate in the survey, but the actions you will take later—based on the survey results—will have more credibility and more general acceptance.

You should publicize the survey in a variety of ways. One idea involves the local media. Meet with them during the planning phase, and explain exactly what the survey intends to do and why. Distribute written materials to those that attend the meeting, as well as those who are unable to attend. Explain the purpose of the survey, the issues to be explored, how the results will be used, and how the survey will be conducted. Use this opportunity to enlist the help of volunteers for the survey project. Have as many people from the survey committee as possible attend this meeting. The local press is usually happy to give space to local citizens in action, and they are likelier to use a picture of the group than of you alone. Distribute a second press release just before the survey is launched, announcing that you are ready to begin. This will raise awareness in the community and hopefully increase cooperation.

Promote the survey in the church bulletin so that all members of the congregation know what is happening. They can then inform their friends and neighbors. If conducting a mail survey, after the questionnaire has been distributed, follow up with announcements from the pulpit or in the bulletin to remind people to return their questionnaires.

Designate one or more people to answer any questions about the survey. Once the survey is completed, it is vital to share the results of the project with the congregation. This helps achieve the second goal of this research endeavor: educating people based on facts gathered through your church survey project.

WHAT SHOULD THE INTERVIEWER DO IF...	RESPOND BY...
respondent asks what a certain word or phrase means?	saying, "Whatever it means for you." If the respondent still refuses to answer, code the response as "don't know/refused."
respondent interrupts during the question with an answer?	recording his or her response unless it does not match response categories; in that case, probe for clarification.
respondent interrupts during the response categories with an answer?	recording his response unless the response categories are on a scale, in which case the interviewer should read all possible answers.
respondent asks for more information?	saying, "If you had to answer on the information you have right now, would you say..." If he or she still refuses to answer without more information, code the response as "don't know/refused."

Chapter Six:

Processing the Questionnaire

DURING A TELEPHONE SURVEY

Assuming that the survey team has trained the interviewers to handle an array of potentially challenging situations, the primary task of the person overseeing this part of the project (called the interview supervisor) is quality control. This involves answering unexpected questions posed to interviewers by respondents, as well as monitoring the progress of interviewers.

We recommend enlisting the help of one or two volunteers who assist with administrative functions while the telephone interviews are underway. The supervisor needs to be free of all administrative distractions so that he or she can pay full attention to the interviewers and answer concerns and questions that arise during the interview process. The administrative volunteers can handle photocopying requests and assistance with questionnaires, as well as review completed questionnaires for any missing information or possible recording errors.

DURING A MAIL SURVEY

As the mail questionnaires are being collected, the job of processing data begins. This consists of three steps: editing, coding, and tabulation. The editing and check-in stage consists of examining the returned questionnaires and preparing them for further processing. First, discard any frivolous questionnaires. These are actually quite rare, but occasionally some jokester will deliberately put down

SURVEY QUALITY CONTROL

Although interviewers faking interviews is highly atypical, especially in situations like a church using its own members to conduct a survey, we recommend that the survey team consider ways to follow up interviews to ensure quality control. Without creating undue suspicion, we suggest that the interview supervisor contact a sample—perhaps 5 or 10 percent—of the total number of respondents to verify their participation in the study via the telephone or mail. We believe that if interviewers are aware of this check on quality, it will serve as a deterrent against any improper behavior.

outrageous or totally contradictory responses. Then, determine if any incomplete questionnaires contain sufficient information on at least the key questions so that they can be included

> ☒ **For mail surveys, we recommend a comprehensive follow-up system to increase the response rate.**

in the results. Next, decide if a respondent is eligible to be in the sample. For example, you might elect to exclude a respondent who writes on the questionnaire, "I am no longer a member of this church" on a membership survey. The next part of the check-in stage relates to inconsistencies. Check the logic of responses and decide how to resolve inconsistencies. For instance, a person who checks "I live alone" and then on another question indicates that there are three people in the household presents an inconsistency that must be resolved. If it is absolutely clear that the person does not live alone, you would change the response during the editing process. If there is no way to tell which answer is correct and there is no other place on the questionnaire that provides the information to resolve this dilemma, a common practice is to change *both* answers to "no response."

Finally, if the interviewer has entered the answer in the wrong place (the respondent has checked an answer category to the right of the categories when he or she has been asked to circle the number that appears to the left of the chosen category), the editor makes the correct marks in the correct place. This will make it likelier that those tabulating the responses will be able to quickly and correctly enter the answers. A thorough review at this stage, although it may appear to be slowing down the process, increases the likelihood that you will analyze valid and consistent data.

QUESTIONNAIRE FOLLOW-UP

For mail surveys, we recommend a comprehensive follow-up system to increase the response rate. You will notice that all correspondence refers to earlier communication, with each piece of communication dated. It is important to mail the letter on the same day it is written in order to maintain the follow-up schedule. If the

LOCATION, LOCATION, LOCATION

We recommend that telephone interviews take place at a central interviewing facility, such as the church office. A central interviewing facility allows the interview supervisor to take over difficult interviews, as well as to answer any questions that arise during the process. A centralized location increases the survey's integrity, making it more difficult for interviewers to falsify information or conduct the interview in a manner that differs from the survey script. It also permits the supervisor to hear the progress of the interviews and to encourage and support the interviewers. If the telephone lines are located in the same room, one practical way to alleviate the noise of other interviews is to place carpeting on the work desks to absorb noise.

surveys were mailed out on Monday, February 1, we recommend the following follow-up system of communication.

 On Monday, Feb. 8: Send a postcard reminder to all respondents. Thank
those who have already responded, and offer a friendly and courteous
reminder for those who have not. These postcards should be printed and
addressed even before the first mailing so that this task does not interfere
with the important task of organizing and reviewing questionnaires as they
arrive in the first week. (See postcard below.)

POSTCARD REMINDER

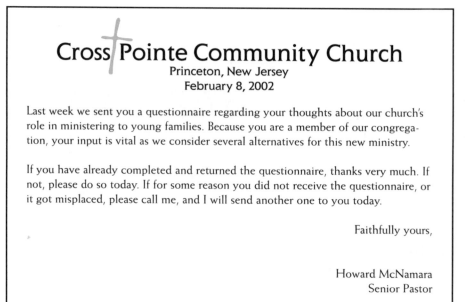

Cross Pointe Community Church
Princeton, New Jersey
February 8, 2002

Last week we sent you a questionnaire regarding your thoughts about our church's
role in ministering to young families. Because you are a member of our congregation, your input is vital as we consider several alternatives for this new ministry.

If you have already completed and returned the questionnaire, thanks very much. If
not, please do so today. If for some reason you did not receive the questionnaire, or
it got misplaced, please call me, and I will send another one to you today.

Faithfully yours,

Howard McNamara
Senior Pastor

 On Monday, Feb. 22: Send a second letter and replacement questionnaire to
those participants who have not yet responded. The cover letter, printed on
the church's letterhead, should be slightly shorter than the cover letter that
accompanied the survey on February 1, and it should have a renewed appeal
for participation. A replacement questionnaire should accompany this second appeal. This second letter should convey a greater degree of insistence
than the first letter. (See letter on page 151.)

 On Monday, March 22: Send a third and final mailing to participants who
have not yet responded. With this third cover letter, also send another
replacement questionnaire, and send both documents via priority or certi-
fied mail. This more expensive form of postage underscores the survey
team's insistence that the participant respond. (See letter on page 152.)

SECOND LETTER

Cross✝Pointe Community Church
Princeton, New Jersey

Office of the Senior Pastor

1 February 22, 2002

Mr. Ron Ward
3434 Purdue Avenue
Princeton, New Jersey 08542

Dear Mr. Ward:

2   About three weeks ago, I wrote to you seeking your opinions and thoughts on a new ministry to young families that our church might undertake in the near future. As of today our survey team has not yet received your completed questionnaire.

3   The church is sponsoring this study because research has shown that a growing number of young families have been moving into the greater Princeton area in recent years. Many churches in the area are considering how to best meet the needs of these young families, and CrossPointe is also seeking input on this decision.

   I am writing you again because every member's participation is essential for the results of this study. In order for the results of this study to be representative of the entire congregation, your participation is vital. In the event that your questionnaire has been misplaced, I am enclosing another copy for you to complete. I appreciate your cooperation very much. We hope to share the results with the entire congregation at our annual spring banquet in May.

Faithfully yours,

 Howard McNamara
Senior Pastor

1. Date mailed
2. Reference to previous correspondence
3. Purpose of the survey
4. Personal signature with name and title

THIRD LETTER

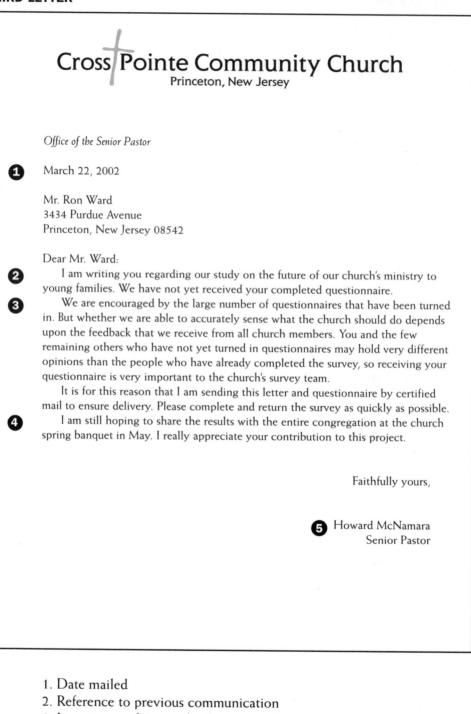

Cross✝Pointe Community Church
Princeton, New Jersey

Office of the Senior Pastor

1 March 22, 2002

Mr. Ron Ward
3434 Purdue Avenue
Princeton, New Jersey 08542

Dear Mr. Ward:

2   I am writing you regarding our study on the future of our church's ministry to young families. We have not yet received your completed questionnaire.

3   We are encouraged by the large number of questionnaires that have been turned in. But whether we are able to accurately sense what the church should do depends upon the feedback that we receive from all church members. You and the few remaining others who have not yet turned in questionnaires may hold very different opinions than the people who have already completed the survey, so receiving your questionnaire is very important to the church's survey team.

    It is for this reason that I am sending this letter and questionnaire by certified mail to ensure delivery. Please complete and return the survey as quickly as possible.

4   I am still hoping to share the results with the entire congregation at the church spring banquet in May. I really appreciate your contribution to this project.

Faithfully yours,

5 Howard McNamara
Senior Pastor

1. Date mailed
2. Reference to previous communication
3. Importance of respondent's participation
4. Reminder of results. Appreciation
5. Personal signature with name and title

CODING

Coding is the process of assigning numbers to the responses given in survey questions. It entails reducing responses to open-ended or free-response questions—such as "What do you think is the most important attribute for our next pastor?"—to categories that summarize the answers. You may have noticed numerical characters or letters beside the response categories on the Gallup surveys provided in this book. These numbers or letters represent codes for each of the responses to close-ended questions. By assigning a numerical value for each response, data analysis can be calculated much more easily, especially using statistical computer packages. However, with open-ended questions, the survey team must establish codes for the various responses offered by the participants. Through this process, hundreds of individual responses usually can be summarized by a half dozen or more general categories or codes. Coding open-ended questions is very time consuming, and constructing the codes is best done by teams, not by one individual, to assure that an answer's essence is correctly captured.

If you are building the codes yourself rather than having a professional survey firm carry out this process, follow these steps:

1. Select eighty to one hundred verbatim responses from the total answers to a given open-ended question, listing them together on a separate sheet of paper.

2. Construct a list of words or concepts that represent the range of answers obtained so that most comments fit into one or another of those groups. This is not a scientific process. It is a trial and error process by which you construct a list, test it, see how you can sharpen the proposed response categories on the preliminary list to make them more appropriate, and consolidate categories or break them apart. Do not be too concerned if you have several responses "left over." Almost every translation of an open-ended answer to a set of response categories contains "Other/miscellaneous" as one of the categories. However, if you find that more than 10 percent of the responses fall into this "other/miscellaneous" category, review those "orphan responses." Another response category that makes sense can probably be created.

3. Prepare a master code sheet for each open-ended question: List each response category followed by a selection of verbatim responses that help the coder understand the kinds of answers that properly belong in that category.

4. Set up a master code sheet such as the sample one below. Notice that we left room in the code for an additional category, which may arise during coding (item 8 on the next page).

SAMPLE MASTER CODE

Most Important Attribute for New Pastor:

    1. dynamic preacher

2. good pastoral counselor

3. strong leader for church staff

4. effective mobilizer for lay leaders

5. strategic visionary for church

6. proven denominational leader

7. intellectually gifted theologian

8.

9. miscellaneous and difficult to classify

10. no opinion/no answer

Do not worry about listing these possible answers in order of importance. The computer can do that later by reporting the number of respondents who chose each category. Always designate one specific code for "don't know/no answer" in order to account for every response.

You are now ready to begin coding. Go through each questionnaire and write the code number given to the open-ended question on the questionnaire. For instance, the coder might assign the number "1" if the respondent talks about health care for senior citizens and then write that number on the questionnaires that give a similar response to the open-ended question. We recommend using a red pen so that the code is easy to spot on the questionnaire. If one respondent gives several answers to the question, write down each of the code numbers on the questionnaire. Continue this process for each open-ended question.

Solicit assistance with the coding process. Designate a team of three or four people for this job, and brief them carefully so that their work is consistent. As a rough guide, assume that four-person hours are required for each one hundred questionnaires, counting the time to build the code. In other words, if you have a team of four people and they each work for one hour, you have allocated enough resources and time to code one open-ended question on one hundred question-naires. Remember to duplicate the master code sheets for each of the workers so that each person has a copy of the codes. We recommend that you code all of the responses to one question during the same "coding session." Assign the numbers to every response on each questionnaire in the margin of the questionnaire using a red pen. Give a code number to questions that were left blank or unanswered so that every question is accounted for when the answers are tabulated. Also, it is important to consult with a computer programmer who will work on the project for placement and format of codes, if tabulating responses by computer.

MULTIPLE CODING

Many respondents will give more than one answer to an open-ended or free-response question. For cases like this, assign numbers to both responses in the margin, as in the following example: 2, 6. When setting up master codes for the open-ended questions, it might be necessary to use more than ten basic categories, which is the limit for one "column" in computer tabulations. One solution is to review the codes to see if there are too many small categories into which

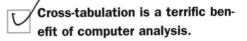
Cross-tabulation is a terrific benefit of computer analysis.

only a few responses will fall. In this situation, consolidate codes. If, indeed, it is essential to have more than ten codes, including "don't know/no answer," then you will need to indicate that two columns must be used. Designate the first group of ten answers as "Column 1" and the second group as "Column 2." This is why professional survey analysts number responses "1, 2, 3,..." if fewer than ten responses exist. However, if there are more than ten responses to the question, the responses will be coded "01, 02, 03...10, 11, 12..."

Codes are not inflexible or static. Even after beginning the coding process, the code categories may expand to reflect the varieties of answers that are falling into the miscellaneous or "other" category. As a rough rule of thumb, if 5 percent of these responses can be grouped together, it is usually best to create a new category. Be sure to tell all of those coding once a new category is created. They will each have to go back over their completed questionnaires and recode that question to accommodate the new category. Obviously, you will want to do this as infrequently as possible. Reducing multiple responses into categories does not mean that the surveyor is discarding important information. You may indicate subtler shades of opinion by quoting verbatim comments within survey results. Be sure to eliminate any reference to individuals or any clues that might reveal the identity of the respondent being quoted.

TABULATION: THE MECHANICS

The next step is to tabulate, or count the answers to questions and determine the totals for analysis. Counting can be done by hand or by computer. If you have surveyed more than one hundred people and if your resources permit, we recommend having the results tabulated by a computer. Hand tabulation is time-consuming and limits the extent to which you can analyze opinions by subgroups (men, women, and people with a college background, among others). Computer tabulation has a number of distinct advantages over hand tabulation, apart from the obvious benefits of speed and efficiency. First, the totals provided by the computer printout will be translated into percents by the computer much more easily. Second, analysis by subgroups of the population surveyed can be computed as easily as the basic totals. Third, responses to one question can be analyzed by responses to other questions; this is called "cross-tabulation." This is a terrific benefit of computer analysis. For instance, the computer can separate out those who say they would be glad to volunteer their time to help the church raise funds and create a table showing the proportion of those potential volunteers who noted that religion is most important in their lives.

If you contract with a professional firm to create computer tabulations, be absolutely certain that they understand and appreciate the complexity of this task. For example, someone who does a great job processing payroll or mailing lists by computer may be completely inexperienced when it comes to survey tabulation. No matter what assurances you receive, if he or she has not done this before, the task may be too daunting.

A local college or university may be able to provide assistance. Often those in the sociology, psychology, political science, or business academic departments have user-friendly computer programs and will be willing to help the church for a consulting fee. The church can also locate a professional firm by looking in the telephone book under a listing such as "marketing research services." It is best to receive two or three competing bids from different professional firms.

If tabulating the results by hand, you will be more limited in the number of characteristics by which you can analyze the results because hand tabulation is so time-consuming. Again, you will need a team of people to complete this task. It is very important to have a clear idea of the kind of information you need before beginning the tabulation stage. Consider different ways the data might be used. Perhaps you will decide that age of the respondent is the most important charac-teristic by which you want to analyze the data. In this case, you would set up a tally sheet with five columns. The first column is for all respondents combined, labeled "All" or "Total." The next four columns might be ages 18-29, 30-49, 50-64, and 65 and older.

The next stage is for the tabulators to review each questionnaire and record the answer given to each question in two places—in the "All" column and also in the age column into which the respondent falls. One way to tabulate the results accu-rately is to first physically divide all of the questionnaires into five stacks—one for each of the age groups if, for instance, you are using age categories as your pri-mary subgroup analytical variable. By doing this, it will not be necessary to check the age category as you tabulate the questionnaires. All those in one pile are in the same age group category.

SAMPLE TALLY SHEET (Using age as the cross-tabulating variable)

Q. 8 Most Important Attribute for New Pastor:	Age				
	All	18-29	30-49	50-64	65 and Older
1. dynamic preacher					
2. good pastoral counselor					
3. strong leader for church staff					
4. effective mobilizer for lay leaders					
5. strategic visionary for church					
6. proven denominational leader					
7. intellectually gifted theologian					
8.					
9. miscellaneous and difficult to classify					
10. no opinion/no answer					

Chapter Seven:

✓ Analyzing the Data

UNDERSTANDING THE DATA

The most important principle to keep in mind as you look over the survey results is that numbers are only a way of standardizing language. That is, they provide a common understanding of what the division of opinion is, but they do not help explain what that division means. If you were to say, for example, "most of the congregation" feels one way rather than another, one listener might think that "most" means everyone but Chris Duperior, who everybody knows is always against everything. Someone else might think that "most" means 90 percent of the congregation. A third person might think that "most" means a little more than half of the congregation. Similarly, if you were to say that the congregation is divided on the issue, one person might think you mean there is a 50-50 division. Someone else might believe that you mean there is a 60-40 split. Still a third person might think that many of the congregants feel one way, but not all of them.

One benefit of a survey, therefore, is that it generates a common language about these issues, although people may disagree on the implications of the findings. Eighty percent always equals eighty percent, and there is no doubting what is at stake when using specific language. What you may now consider is whether 80 percent can be described as "most," "many," or "a lot." And you are still left with the task of deciding on the point at which you have a mandate to act. Is it at the point where 51 percent of the congregation feels a certain way? sixty percent? eighty percent? ninety-five percent?

Thus, in a survey of a relatively small group, as we are assuming is your situation, you should view the numbers primarily as a guide to congregational sentiment. A finding that 80 percent of the congregation feel one way is about the same as a finding that 75 percent or 90 percent feel that way. Each of these three possible findings helps church leaders understand the direction of congregational thinking, whether the number is called "a lot," "many," or "most" of the congregation.

☒ **Very rarely can a pastor find large groups of parishioners that hold the same opinion on several different issues.**

The second principle to keep in mind is that the division of opinion on one issue may be viewed differently than the divisions of opinion on other issues. Very rarely can a pastor find large groups of parishioners that hold

☑ **Conducting a survey is the easy part of your task. Understanding how to use the findings prudently is the hard part.**

the same opinion on several different issues. This is important when designing the survey and analyzing the results. You must be attentive to the responses of each question and make sure that all of the major concerns are addressed in the questionnaire. For instance, the decision to undertake building a new sanctuary for the church should be supported by "a lot" of the congregation, whether you decide that "a lot" means 65 percent, 75 percent, or 95 percent. Without the firm backing of the congregation, you will not have its support in the challenge of fund raising.

Therefore, it is important to ask specific questions in the questionnaire and to analyze the data carefully. Conducting a survey is the easy part of your task. Understanding how to use the findings prudently is the hard part, for which there are no magical rules.

CONSTRUCTING TABLES

Before analyzing the data and preparing a report, first simplify the mass of numerical data by percentaging. If the survey tabulation was done by computer (or Scantron or some other mechanical method), you will already have percentages. If not, convert all the basic figures into percentage totals. For example, if you find that 193 people of those who participated in the survey (372) feel one way and 179 feel another way, percentages can be very helpful in analyzing the results. While it is clear that there are more in one group than in the other, it is somewhat more revealing to see that the 193 represent only 52 percent—a slim majority.

Percentages not only make numerical findings easier to read, but they also make it easier to understand the relationships. For example, you might want to compare how longtime members of the congregation feel about some issue with how newcomers to the church feel about that issue. When looking at their responses separately, these results, expressed in numbers, might appear:

	All	Longtime Members	New Members
Yes	193	122	71
No	179	112	67
All	372	234	138

While you can easily see that among both groups, more members approve than disapprove of the issue, you might not have grasped immediately that the same *proportion* of each group approves of the issue. Seeing the results expressed as percentages helps you see this. "N" represents the raw number counted for each subsection of the survey. Here is how the same results look, transformed into percentages:

	All	Longtime Members	New Members
N=	(372)	(234)	(138)
Yes	52%	52%	52%
No	48%	48%	48%
All	100%	100%	100%

In some cases, you may decide that you want to show both the actual questionnaire counts and the percentages side-by-side. In this case your table would look like this:

	All		Longtime Members		New Members	
	N		N		N	
Yes	193	52%	122	52%	71	52%
No	179	48%	112	48%	67	48%
All	372	100%	234	100%	138	100%

If the survey committee includes some members who are skilled with using the computer, you may be able to show some of your findings in graphic form, such as bar graphs and pie charts.

For ease of analysis, round percentages to the nearest whole number. For one thing, there is no such creature as 0.7 percent of a person. Also, tables that include percents carried to one or more decimal places are harder to read. In addition, reporting tables in tenths or hundredths conveys a sense of greater accuracy than is supported by the data. Survey data contains several types of "inaccuracies." Not everyone who participates in the survey pays close attention to every question. Those responding to the questionnaire might lose their attention, and they might not know exactly how they feel on a particular matter. If you were to ask them again tomorrow, they might answer differently. As a result, "human error" is always present in a survey. And of course, every survey that relies on a sample rather than on everyone in the universe has a margin of error. Thus, 52 percent is, in effect, an approximation—perhaps a good approximation, but an approximation nonetheless.

What should one do with figures such as 27.4? Is it 27 or 28? What about 27.6? There are a number of rounding conventions, and one can justify any of them. What is important is to select one and stick with it, so that all the tables have been constructed in the same way. Two rounding conventions prevail within the field of survey research. According to one of the models, if a response is .4 or less, round it down to the nearest whole number; if it is .5 or greater, round it up to the nearest whole number. Using this typology, our example of 27.4 percent would be rounded to 27 percent. A second model states that if a response is less than .5, round down to the nearest whole number. Similarly, if the percent is .6 or greater, round up. The difference, then, between the two rounding conventions relates to those figures

that are exactly .5. This second convention follows a more complicated rule: The figure should be rounded up to the nearest whole number if the basic percent is odd-numbered (27.5 percent becomes 28 percent) and keep

> ☑ **For the powerful advantage of cross-tabulations, we recommend using the computer for tabulation, if at all possible.**

it at the basic percent if that is even (28.5 percent becomes 28 percent). For the sake of simplicity, we prefer the first rounding convention. It is easier to remember, and most of us recall it from elementary math classes. However, both rounding conventions are acceptable; the key is consistency. Choose a model and stick with it.

Sometimes tables may not add exactly to 100 percent. On occasion, this will be the result of rounding percentages. However, if the tables add to less than 99 percent or more than 101 percent, recheck the arithmetic; rounding should not produce more than one percentage point more or less than 100. Tables will also add to more than 100 percent when more than one answer is allowed for a particular question. If, for instance, survey participants are asked to name all of the factors that influenced their decision to join the church, the total percentages will obviously total more than 100.

WATCH OUT FOR SMALL BASES

As a general rule, if the number of people in a group is less than about fifty, you should display your findings in numbers instead of percentages. With a small group, a change of only a few answers produces a wide swing in the percentages, which is often misleading.

CROSS-TABULATIONS

Cross-tabulating means simply comparing the answers to one question with those of another. The example of comparing longtime members and new members is actually a cross-tabulation that compares two types of members on one issue based upon their answers to one of the questions. The computer makes these types of comparisons much easier to produce, and we encourage computer-based tabulations for this reason. By building a database on the computer that records every person's responses, the survey team can generate numerous statistics that compare demographic information with responses to certain questions. For example, you could query the computer database to report how many female respondents compared to male respondents favored building a new children's wing at the church. After noting how many men and women—in terms of both raw number counts and percentages—are in favor of this proposal, you could create a report that queries the number of younger adults compared to older adults in the

church in favor of the new children's wing. The computer can produce these calculations within minutes; however, hand-tabulated figures can take hours, sometimes even days. For the powerful advantage of cross-tabulations, we recommend using the computer for tabulation, if at all possible.

THE LANGUAGE OF THE REPORT

In preparing the text of the report, great care must be taken not to overstate the findings. The term *majority*, as an example, can be misleading in a survey report. While 51 percent is a majority, so is 81 percent. Here are some guidelines for describing results.

PERCENT THAT APPROVE OF A PARTICULAR ISSUE	PERCENT THAT DISAPPROVE OF THE SAME ISSUE	PERCENT WHO HAVE NO OPINION ON THE ISSUE	SUGGESTED STATEMENT
45%	45%	10%	evenly divided
48%	45%	7%	about evenly divided
51%-54%	49%-46%		a small majority
55%-59%	45%-41%		a majority
60%-74%	40%-26%		a strong majority
75%-94%	25%-5%		most
95% or more	less than 5%		virtually all

WHAT IS WORTH REPORTING?

This question has to be answered in two ways: One is the answer that is appropriate to a statistician versed in probability statistics; the other is the answer that is appropriate to a lay group working on a survey. If the team is planning a survey that relies on a carefully drawn sample and they are guided by a research professional, that person can guide you on the intricacies of what is "statistically significant." This manual cannot include the amount of detail that is necessary to guide you without on-site statistical help. If, however, you are working as a group of lay surveyors, here are some general guidelines that may help you in deciding what is worth reporting.

◆ Do not use the language of the statistician; that is, do not describe your findings as "significant." This might convey more rigor than is appropriate.

◆ The popular media like to dramatize results, and they usually focus on differences among groups. However, in most congregational surveys, identifying the areas of consensus is important, if not more important than the issues that divide the church. Look for the questions on which there is a high degree of consensus (as many as 75 percent or more choosing one answer over others). These will be important building blocks for strengthening the community within the congregation.

◆ Although you are interested in the issues on which there is consensus and difference of opinion among various subgroups of the congregation, begin the analysis with a sense of the opinions and attitudes of the congregation as a whole.

◆ Even on issues where a strong majority exists (60 percent or more), remain sensitive to the possibility that there is a small group that feels isolated from the congregation as a whole and whose answers consistently fall into the "losing" side. Here is where a separate look at the subgroups of the congregation can be helpful, such as the newer members of the church or those who are older members of the congregation.

◆ Do not make too much of small differences. Remember, this survey is not trying to predict the outcome of a national election. If 68 percent of the congregation says that choral music during worship services is very important to them personally, and 65 percent says that about congregational hymns and responses, this is about the same proportion. It would be a mistake to make much of a difference of three percentage points, particularly since your margin of error is likely to be three points, if not more. Begin talking about differences of opinion where at least five percentage points separate the two opinions. Do not become highly interested in noting differences until they are at least nine or ten percentage points.

A WORD ABOUT GENERALIZABILITY

The goal of the survey, of course, is to provide valid, reliable information upon which churches can base important decisions. However, the survey team must be careful about the extent to which the results of its survey can be generalized. For example, if the church surveys parents of young children about their attitudes regarding the children's ministry of the church, the survey team must be mindful that the survey results do not necessarily reflect the opinions of the entire church. Survey researchers call this "generalizability" to refer to the extent to which conclusions drawn from a surveyed group are true for an entire population.

Chapter Eight:

✓ Reporting the Results and Taking Action

A s the end of the survey process nears, reflect on objectives identified at the start of the project. Although careful analysis of the data is important, your report will require commentary on the implications of the findings. You may choose to integrate this commentary into the body of the report or to preface the report with a section labeled "Implications of the Findings."

MEETING THE NEEDS OF YOUR READERS

First, include a summary. When you have completed writing the entire report, produce a one- or two-page summary of the major findings. Many readers will want to know "the big picture," but they will not want to read the entire report. You may consider reproducing this summary in the church newsletter, with the full report available to those who would like the details.

Second, create a report that appeals to those readers who are comfortable with figures, as well as those who are not. Some people enjoy reading tables, graphs, and pages of statistical data. Others prefer narrative explanations. Draft a report that appeals to both of them. A style that is often used by professionals in the research field is to lead off in the first sentence or paragraph with a prose state-ment of the finding, followed by some sentences or a paragraph with numeral results. They follow this dual-presentation approach with a table or a graph. Here is an example:

Most new members characterize the congregation as "very friendly." In our sur-vey of those who have been members for less than two years, almost three-quar-ters of the new members describe the church as "very friendly." When asked to describe the congregation, 73 percent of those who have been members for less than two years chose "very friendly," with 18 percent saying "somewhat friendly" and 9 percent choosing "not too friendly." None of these new members say that the congregation is "not at all friendly." Women are even likelier than men to give the congregation the highest rating of "very friendly."

The table on page 164 shows these results.

Perception of Friendliness of Congregation by New Members

NEW MEMBERS	ALL	MEN	WOMEN
N=	138	64	74
very friendly	73%	68%	82%
friendly	18%	20%	14%
not too friendly	9%	12%	4%
not at all friendly	0%	0%	0%
Total	100%	100%	100%

VERBATIM COMMENTS

Earlier in the text, we reviewed the process of clustering the answers to open-ended questions into groups so that they can be tabulated similar to close-ended question tabulations. You may also want to follow this table with a selection of verbatim comments from which you constructed the table. They will give the readers insight into the types of ideas that undergird respondents' answers. You may choose to include the entire list of comments in the main text or in the appendix. Often, the responses to the final "what else do you want to tell us" questions do not lend themselves to coding. Because the respondents are being invited to address anything on their minds, the responses can be extremely diverse. Listing all of these comments is almost always useful, even if they are grouped into categories.

These are conventions of the field of survey research, and Christian practitioners ought to follow these ethical principles with the greatest attention and to the highest degree.

ELEMENTS OF THE REPORT
PREFACE OR LETTER OF TRANSMITTAL

On occasion, it is appropriate for a church official to preface the report with a letter or statement that sets forth the significance of the study and the need to implement the findings, to highlight favorable results, or to point out areas that need improvement based on the data.

INTRODUCTION

State the objectives of the survey and answer the following questions.
1. What group was studied, and how were members chosen (census or sampling method)?
2. What was the response rate (the percentage of the group that returned the completed questionnaires or granted interviews)?
3. How was the study conducted (in-person, mail questionnaire, self-administered questionnaire answered during Sunday school, telephone interviews)?
4. When did the data collection start, and when did it end?

5. Who conducted the survey (acknowledge committee members, volunteer groups, and any outside consultants or suppliers who have played a key role)?

SUMMARY OF PRINCIPAL FINDINGS AND RECOMMENDATIONS

Not everyone will have the interest to read the entire report. Provide a concise overview of the findings. If appropriate, also include a summary of the recommendations or implications derived from the findings.

A WORD ABOUT ETHICS

 Christian leaders must take great care in producing the survey report. A well-constructed report that outlines the steps taken and clearly presents the findings is a vital help if the survey is to be repeated sometime in the future. You are not required to release the findings of the survey, but the ethics of survey reporting follow a certain standard: If you release *some* of the findings, you should make *all* of the findings available. Specifically, it would offer an incomplete picture if just the "good news" was released. Recipients of the survey results have the right to expect all of the results if any of the data is released, and the presenters of the results have the obligation to provide it.

Additionally, survey researchers are bound by ethics to refuse the release of names and addresses of survey respondents to anyone outside the survey team unless survey respondents give permission. Interviewers must endorse the ethical obligation to keep respondents' answers and comments in strict confidence. Whenever reporting individual respondents' comments or answers, the surveyor must never include the name or address of the respondent with his or her answer (unless permission is granted). Furthermore, survey researchers must be careful to present tabulations in broad enough categories that individual respondents cannot be singled out. Consider the following ideas for maintaining the highest levels of ethical integrity with your survey project.

◆ Every person who will have access to the data or a role in collecting the data must agree to maintain confidentiality.

◆ Remove any names or identification numbers from questionnaires as soon as possible in order to eliminate the possibility of connecting a particular individual with a questionnaire.

◆ Notice the number of observations for a given questionnaire item (that is, the number of responses). Small numbers of observations should be reported with care so that respondents are not identified by particular findings from the survey.

REPORT FINDINGS IN DETAIL

Show tables with the exact question wording and results. The report should also provide a short paragraph or two describing the table. Finally, verbatim comments from open-ended questions should, when available, also accompany the detailed findings. Remember that verbatim comments can be grouped into distinguishing categories such as "new members" and "longtime members."

METHODOLOGY REPORT

Since the survey team has taken considerable care in designing the survey's methodology, you should include certain important elements in the final report, such as

- method and timing (month, year) of data collection (mail, telephone, in-person interviews);
- quality control: panel of experts, pretesting, interview debriefing, revision, callbacks for nonrespondents (How many times did the team attempt to reach participants? What was the rate of response?);
- profile of *unit* non-response (people who did not participate) and information about *item* non-response (particular questions that were problematic);
- description of methods used for follow-up in attempting to reduce unit non-response;
- length of time to complete each survey and span of time from beginning to end of survey project;
- characteristics of the survey administrators and interviewers (volunteers or professionals), as well as their training in survey research (one-day seminar or semester-long course); and
- editing and coding questionnaires for data analysis.

CHECKLIST FOR WRITING A REPORT

- ◆ Are the survey's main objectives stated clearly?

- ◆ Does the report acknowledge the organization that sponsors the study, as well as note the names of survey team members and others involved in some stage of the project?

- ◆ Are the total number of questions and their exact wording included?

- ◆ Are the response categories for each item on the questionnaire included, as well as descriptions of codes used for open-ended questions?

- ◆ Does the report explain the method of data collection, its strengths and shortcomings for this particular project, and the length of time required for data collection?

- ◆ Is the number of survey participants listed, as well as the number of people who refused to participate? Does the report describe the characteristics of people who refused to cooperate?

- ◆ Are the methods for ensuring reliability (quality control) explained?

CONCLUSION

Summarize and interpret the results, and explain how they fit into the context of the survey's objectives. Discuss the limitations of the survey's design, as well as to what extent the results from this survey can be generalized to other populations. Conclude with the most significant findings and how they bear on future actions of the church and its leadership.

APPENDIX

The appendix is the appropriate place for background materials such as a copy of the entire questionnaire; a statistical profile of the respondents; and, when indicated, a map of the area surveyed.

USING CHARTS AND GRAPHS

Pie charts, bar and line graphs, and other illustrative material can add pizazz to any final report. One of the most important elements of any chart or graph of statistical data is the chart's scale. The scale refers to the numbers that mark the increments on one of the axes, and often the y-axis is the one to notice. If someone wants to change the relative importance of a graph—either by making it more alarming or less significant—the y-axis scale is the easiest place to shape the readers' perception. For example, consider the following graph (Graph 1) comparing the importance of religion in the United States and the New England region.

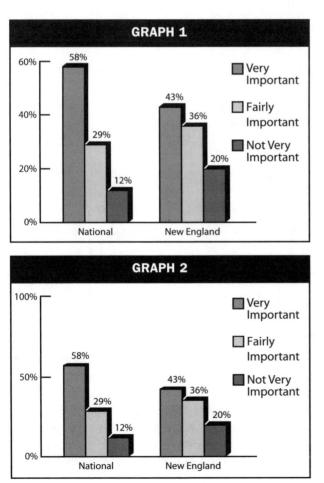

Now if we change the scale of the y-axis, notice the remarkably different appearance of the data (Graph 2).

The data have not changed, but their relative importance has been significantly modified by simply changing the scale of the y-axis.

Use pie charts to express proportions or percentages. Pie charts are usually not a

good way to present comparisons, but they are excellent for illustrating the relation of one segment of the population to another. For example, pie charts are excellent when illustrating the percentage of people who respond with different answers to the same question. In the example shown, Gallup asked Americans, "How would you describe yourself—as religious or as spiritual but not religious?"

Whenever using a graph in the final report, keep these suggestions in mind:

◆ Give each graph a short, succinct title.

◆ If necessary, group small elements together and label them as "other." Description is often more important than precision when using graphs in a survey report.

◆ Do not include more than eight categories of response in a single graph; otherwise, the graph is too difficult to comprehend.

◆ Explain the meaning of the values on the x-axis and the y-axis.

◆ Provide a key or legend.

◆ Always include source information if the report will be distributed to the media or individuals outside the church. The graphs should state the total number of people surveyed, the date of the survey, where it was conducted, and who commissioned the survey project.

MINIMUM REPORTING REQUIREMENTS

Any public release of the survey data should be accompanied by the following vital information:

1. Who sponsored the survey? What was the survey's overall purpose?

2. Who were the respondents (description of qualifications, not actual names)?

3. How many people were interviewed?

4. Where did the survey take place?

5. How was it done? What type of survey methodology (self-administered, in-person, or telephone) was employed?

6. If it is a sample of the population, what are the sampling tolerances?

This can usually be done in one paragraph, as in the following examples:

The George H. Gallup International Institute conducted this survey for Christian Ministry Resources in the fall of 2002. The survey was conducted by telephone among a nationally representative sample of 1007 American adults age eighteen and older. Interviewing took place during October, 2002. For the sample as a whole, differences of 3 percentage points or more are statistically significant—that is, are not attributable to sampling error. The Appendix contains a table of sampling tolerances that identifies the differences in subgroup responses that are attributable to sampling error and those that are statistically significant.

When the survey project is completed, give thought to what items should be kept for future surveys.

ARCHIVES

When the survey project is completed, give thought to what items should be kept for future surveys. We recommend that you save the completed questionnaires for one or two years. Questions regarding the survey may arise that can be answered only by returning to the questionnaires. You may want to throw them away after two years because it is unlikely they will be needed or will still be relevant after that time. Also, you may wish to save the list of those to whom you distributed the questionnaire until it becomes too obsolete. Until then, it may

---

COMPUTER SLIDE SHOWS

 In today's technologically savvy world, we recommend the use of a software package that creates electronic slide shows for presenting the survey team's final report. Microsoft PowerPoint and several other packages can be used to create eye-catching graphics that keep viewers' attention. We have used these computer-generated slide shows many times, and we offer the following recommendations:

1. Limit each slide to a single item on the questionnaire.

2. Create one slide for every one to two minutes of a presentation; for a thirty-minute presentation, create a slide show of fifteen to thirty slides.

3. Use no more than seven to nine lines of text per slide and no more than seven words per line.

4. Use phrases instead of complete sentences.

5. Keep the font size larger than eighteen point.

6. Use dark, cool colors for slide backgrounds (blue is regarded as the most professional) and bright, warm colors for slide text (white is easiest to read on a dark background).

7. Use slide transitions and build animations to keep the presentation lively.

8. Round numbers to the nearest whole number; no one knows what .4 of a person represents.

9. Run spell-checker several times before the presentation; a misspelled word that is broadcast on a large screen can be very embarrassing!

10. Avoid using several font styles. Keep the graphics and color schemes consistent throughout the presentation.

represent your most up-to-date list of the group you studied and may prove useful for projects such as updating the stewardship drive list or updating the list of
those who receive the church's weekly newsletter. We further recommend that
you save a file of the materials that would allow you or someone else to repeat all
or part of the study several years from now. This should include blank copies of
the questionnaire, a description of the sample and how it was drawn, the budget,
the schedule, and instructions to volunteers. It is also helpful to include a note on
what you would have done differently after completing one entire survey "cycle."
Save copies of any data disks that may be used for further analysis, as well as
copies of reports on computer disks that contain the reports. Finally, a copy of
the overall report should become a part of the church's permanent archives. One
hundred years from now, members will be fascinated with the results!

TAKING ACTION

A survey is not worth undertaking unless it leads to specific action steps. Too
often, lay groups put the survey report on the shelf for later discussions, which
sometimes can mean it never receives thoughtful consideration. While it takes a
great deal of effort to mobilize for action, it is the last stage that offers the greatest payoff. Do not neglect it.

We recommend a meeting of the survey team to review the findings and to discuss them. You might want to precede the meeting with time for the committee to
plan prospective strategies. Prepare an outline for taking action on results and use
the findings to guide the group's thinking. The use of survey findings has probably
been determined prior to the launching of the survey. Here are some possible uses:

1. internal guidance with results kept confidential.

2. informing members through bulletins, newsletters, seminars, sermons, and
special meetings.

3. presentation to local clergy groups or denomination leaders.

4. presentation to the media—locally or nationally. In such cases, it is important to have copies of the full report and key findings available.

5. If appropriate, forward copies of the report to the regional and national
offices of your church.

6. Is it appropriate to form subcommittees to plan strategies for action? Begin
while the survey findings are fresh in everyone's mind. Is it more appropriate
for staff to develop plans? Again, begin this as soon as possible. Translate
the survey findings and their implications into a specific strategy plan.

However you use the survey findings, they should help address the deeper
questions that led to its undertaking. What are the strengths upon which a church
should build? What are the major challenges? What steps need to be taken to deal
with these strengths and these challenges? What specific steps can be undertaken
to deepen the faith of the parishioners? What can be done to maintain a productive balance between inner renewal and social renewal?

Afterword

If you have reached this point in the guide, your eyes are probably glazed over from looking at all the lists of do's and don'ts. While these reminders are of course included to help you avoid unsuspected pitfalls, you may feel nervous about taking the plunge and launching a survey, particularly if this is the first time you have attempted such a project.

However, if you and your associates feel that a survey would, indeed, shed important light on issues of concern and you have developed a solid working team, you probably will not encounter any major problems. Be sure on your first time out to keep your questions simple and few in number. And you may want to pilot or pretest the survey on, say, twenty or thirty persons just to be sure that all the pieces of the survey are in working order. Then, based on this experience, move forward with the larger survey.

You will learn a great deal in the "doing" of a survey, and the next time around you will be a real pro. It is probably a good idea not to undertake a new survey right away, so as not to burden members of your church—unless, of course, there are specific issues that call for an immediate before-and-after measurement.

Ideally, a survey should lead to positive action steps being taken on the basis of survey findings. You will need to reconvene your working team to discuss ways to use the survey results to best advantage.

You may want to use the findings only for internal guidance (if so, you should let this be known before the survey is launched). If you plan to report the findings to the congregation as a whole, there are, of course, a number of ways to do this—through church bulletins, newsletters, seminars, in sermons, at the annual meeting, and so forth.

Perhaps you may wish to present the findings to local clergy groups or denominational leaders. And you may feel it would be useful to offer the survey results to the local media. If so, you will need to bear in mind that the media will likely want access to the full report.

Once the data is in hand and analyzed, the information can be shared with various committees to use as a basis for strategic action in terms of the focus of these committees—outreach, building and grounds, spiritual growth, and the like.

Presenting the key findings to the entire congregation in a visually appealing presentation is, of course, a way to build support and enthusiasm for key action steps.

This guide offers a creative and modern way to listen to the people you serve, not only recording the division of opinion on key issues, but at the same time determining responses to a range of options or alternatives to proposals and plans.

Surveys on religion have been sometimes decried as supporting "leadership by consensus" instead of "prophetic leadership." Indeed, it is important that leaders *lead* and not *follow* public opinion. But by the same token, leaders should know all they can about the people they are trying to lead because prophetic leadership does not rule out the possibility that God is leading or speaking through his people.

Leaders need reality checks to know where their people are in core beliefs and in their faith journeys. And if we believe God speaks to people, then it becomes important to measure their response—to get a sense of his purposes by a sense of where people are in their faith journeys.

The tribe of Issachar "understood the times and knew what Israel should do." We, too, need to use every tool at our disposal—including scientific survey research—to gain insight into God's purpose for his people in today's world, by letting them speak through the mechanism of scientific surveys.

Appendix:
Statistical Sampling

The following guidelines apply to surveys when only some part of the population—a sample—is being queried, not when surveying all of one group. One fundamental rule of statistical sampling is that the sample must be representative. The word *representative* has a very precise meaning in the arena of statistical surveying; namely, that every individual in the population has an equal and known chance of being included in the sample. This may appear to be a relatively simple rule to follow, but consider these potential pitfalls.

Suppose your congregation includes one thousand people, and the survey team decides to survey a sample of one hundred. The team selects the one hundred by taking every fifth person on the list. However, there are two difficulties with this method. The first defect comes from the way in which the sample was selected— the sample of one hundred people will be complete by the time you reach person number five hundred. Those who are numbered 501 through 1000 had no chance of being selected. One may avoid this difficulty by dividing the total number of people on the list—one thousand in this case—by the number wanted for sample selection—one hundred—and counting forward by the result—ten—to find the next sample candidate.

Notice the second defect: persons one through nine also have no chance of being selected since the team began with the tenth person on the list. To avoid this problem, select a random number (every statistics text contains a Table of Random Numbers, which is a series of numbers generated in random sequence by a computer; also most computer spreadsheet applications have a random function that can produce similar results). The random number should have as many digits as the survey's "universe"—the total number of people from whom the survey team will be sampling. If the first number in the Table of Random Numbers is, say, 014, begin the count with the fourteenth person on the list. If the first number in the Table of Random Numbers is 889, begin the count with the 889th person and continue counting forward by ten (cycling around the one thousandth person to the first person on the list) until reaching the target one hundred people.

This type of sampling is called a "systematic sample," which is often used in surveys among small populations. Larger-scale surveys use a different method called probability sampling, the intricacies of which are beyond the scope of this book (and of most church's probable needs or resources). Drawing a statistically representative sample will reflect the characteristics of the congregation in about the same proportions as they exist. That is, if the church is comprised of a mix of older and younger people, the sample will contain that mix as well. If the congregation is comprised predominantly of older people, that will be the character of the sample as well.

How large a sample is needed? If the proper procedures are followed, a sample of, say, three hundred people will reflect the views of a congregation of one thousand or five thousand or ten thousand with a high degree of accuracy. National polls, for example, typically use samples of one thousand to represent the views of the hundreds of millions of adults. In fact, there are statistical formulas for determining how accurately a statistical sample reflects the universe, if the team has drawn a sample following the proper procedures. Reports from professional surveys always include a statement documenting the range of accuracy, called a "sampling error." These statements typically read: "The results obtained in this survey are accurate within plus or minus 3 percentage points (or whatever percent reflects the sample size) at the 95 percent level of confidence." In everyday language, this means that if someone interviewed the entire universe, the chances are 95 out of 100 that the results from the sample will be within 3 percentage points of the "true" results, plus or minus. Or stated another way, if the survey were repeated many times using the same sampling procedures, the same questionnaire, and within the same time period, one could expect the results to vary by the stated percentage (3 percentage points, for instance) 95 percent of the time. The smaller the sample, the larger the range of "sampling error." The larger the sample, the smaller the range of "sampling error."

The answer to the question of how large a sample is needed, therefore, is not a question of sample size but a question of how much "sampling error" the surveyor can accept. If someone is trying to predict who will win a Presidential election, where the results are sometimes as close as 49 percent for one candidate and 51 percent for the winner, he will not be happy with a sampling error of +5 percentage points. On the other hand, if someone is trying to determine the level of support within the congregation for the next fund drive, a sampling error of +5 percentage points is close enough. If the success of the fund drive depends on the support of an extra 5 percent of the congregation, you are facing an uphill battle!

A second major consideration in determining sample size is the question of how the team wants to use the information once collected. Are church leaders going to analyze the data looking only at the congregation as a whole? In that case, a sample of two hundred to three hundred is an adequate minimum sample. However, if you want to divide respondents in different ways, say men versus women or older congregants versus younger people, then a larger sample may be needed so that the sample bases for the smaller groups are large enough to provide projectional information. A good general rule of thumb is that one should have at least fifty people from each group the surveyor wants to analyze, regardless of the size of the sample. To compare men versus women, a sample of one hundred is needed to obtain about fifty of each. To compare older men and women versus younger men and women, a sample of two hundred is needed to obtain about fifty older men, fifty older women, fifty younger men, and fifty younger women.

Group Publishing, Inc.
Attention: Product Development
P.O. Box 481
Loveland, CO 80539
Fax: (970) 679-4370

Evaluation for
The Gallup Guide

Please help Group Publishing, Inc., continue to provide innovative and useful resources for ministry. Please take a moment to fill out this evaluation and mail or fax it to us. Thanks!

● ● ●

1. As a whole, this book has been (circle one)

not very helpful   very helpful

1   2   3   4   5   6   7   8   9   10

2. The best things about this book:

3. Ways this book could be improved:

4. Things I will change because of this book:

5. Other books I'd like to see Group publish in the future:

6. Would you be interested in field-testing future Group products and giving us your feedback? If so, please fill in the information below:

Name_____

Church Name _____

Denomination _____ Church Size _____

Church Address _____

City _____ State _____ ZIP _____

Church Phone _____

E-mail _____

Permission to photocopy this page granted for local church use.
Copyright © Group Publishing, Inc., P.O. Box 481, Loveland, CO 80539. www.grouppublishing.com